Fierce Woman Inspirational

Natalie Blake

Ready Media LLC

Fierce Woman Inspirational

Publisher: READY Media LLC
www.ReadyPublication.com

Printed in the United States of America

ISBN: 978-1-7358073-1-7

Table of Contents

Book Dedication

This book is dedicated to my mother, who has the most beautiful soul of any woman that I have ever met. You give of yourself tirelessly with the biggest smile on your face. You radiate beauty wherever you go, and people are drawn to your kind heart. I can only hope to be half the woman that you are one day: strong, caring, loving and beautiful inside and out. I am so proud to be your daughter. Thank you for making me the fierce woman I was meant to be!

FORWARD

It was many years ago, but I remember it like it was yesterday. The first time Natalie and I met is still clear in my mind. We met at a restaurant after a mutual friend suggested that we might have some common interests. And that blind date was the start of the rest of my life!

That night, after an icebreaker, our connection seemed like it had already been there for years. Our personalities, our interests, our loves, our fears and a slew of other similarities created an immediate bond. A connection made even stronger by Natalie's infectious laugh, her brilliant smile and her radiant beauty.

Several years of marriage brought us boundless adventures, numerous concerts, magnificent travels and even new business ventures. As we went from one to another, we kept getting led to other adventures or opportunities. And this is where our honeymoon to Italy comes into the story. We both knew that our trip to Italy was going to be an amazing journey. It was there that we naturally fell in love with the look, the feel and the style of Italian purses. So much so that we actually had to buy an extra piece of luggage to bring them back home. And rightly so! Each and every purse has an elegance and style that you simply cannot replicate elsewhere. And with that came the "off the cuff" idea of starting an American purse company that sells genuine Italian leather handbags. With our busy schedules, that idea lingered in the background of our minds but was never forgotten.

That idea finally made its way to reality after a chance meeting with Cameron at Rockwell Tharp. A brief stop into his retail store in Florida turned into a long conversation about how he and Kristi started their business. Cameron shared with us their stories of how they made it through the trials and tribulations of a start-up business. And it was those stories that inspired us to take the chance—a leap of faith into the creation of The Natty Girl Company: a company dedicated to bringing the style and feel of Italian leather purses to the American market. But that's not the end of the story...

As Natalie and I worked to figure out how to name and market these purses, she came up with the idea that we would name each Italian purse after an inspirational woman in our lives. And with the naming of the purse, she asked each inspirational woman to share her story as a way to inspire other women. The stories came in, and the tears went out! We were flabbergasted with what these amazing women were sharing! Women, whom we had known for years, were sharing stories about their lives that we had never known about. Stories that left us speechless and awe-struck! They have exemplified such courage in sharing these stories in the hopes that other women will be inspired, comforted, consoled or even restored by their words.

And it was with that goal—to help other women—that drove Natalie to set upon this adventure. An adventure that has been so exciting to watch. I have been by her side laughing and crying as she works with the women in this book. The stories started coming in one after another, with each one being more incredible than the last. Some of the stories are sad and give you appreciation. Others make you laugh. Others make you cry and fill your heart with understanding. I can go on and on, but what I found is that every one of these stories have touched Natalie and me. It was all these brave women who gave Natalie the drive and the courage to keep this project going. Yes, I may have lent a hand towards that goal too, but these brave ladies get the credit.

Thank you, Natalie, for bringing this project to print. I know that this book will help more women than you could ever imagine! You are truly an amazing and inspirational person!

Your loving husband,

Kevin

P.S.: If you should have the chance to meet Natalie in person, make sure to ask her about the icebreaker on our first date. You will get to experience her infectious laugh and brilliant smile.

Acknowledgments

I am humbly grateful to God for putting that inner light, that spark, that fire inside of me that would not let me rest until I wrote this book. Thanks for making me so uncomfortable at night that I could not sleep because I knew the pain of not writing it would be greater than the fear of failure, shame and disappointment I could receive by writing it. You pushed me through my uncomfortable zones of fear and the unknown, to say the least!

Secondly, I want to thank my husband for pushing me through my whining, hesitancy and negative self-talk, as I said, "I can't do this, it's too hard and no one will want to read it." He was amazingly supportive and pushed me through self-doubt, as I hope these devotionals will do for you!

Thirdly, I would like to thank all these amazingly strong, fierce women for being part of this devotional. You have opened your hearts, hurts, accomplishments and visions for other women to help pave a way for their success in life. You have inspired me to become a better person and have pushed me to help inspire and uplift other women.

Lastly to my family, friends and Savvy Publishing, who pushed me through self-doubt and helped me keep marching forward! You are the true blessings in my life!

And a special thank you to all of you who have bought this book and are starting your own journey. I wish you peace, love and the courage to never give up! Always let your higher power help you put one foot in front of the other and carry you through the hard times and **be the fierce woman you were meant to be.**

Note From the Author

Choose to live the "What If"

What if you saw things in a different light?
How would you wake up? Enthusiastic? Grateful? Sad?
I guess it depends on how you see it, right?

So, let's say you wake up and you hop on the scale and learn you have dropped a couple of pounds. That always makes me feel good! Wouldn't you feel positive and want to start the day continuing down that same path? You would probably go exercise right away, choose to eat the right breakfast and make good choices the rest of the day.

So, I challenge you to try the "What If" experiment for one whole day! Challenge yourself to step out of your box and take positive action towards your dreams and goals for one day. Think of all the "what-ifs" in your life, and just do them! Maybe it is joining a gym, taking a class, asking that special someone out on a date, looking for a new job or just telling your family you love them.

Choose to wake up with a positive light! A light so bright no one can extinguish it. Choose to think positive thoughts and watch tiny miracles happen all day!

Today, will you will choose to step out of your comfort zone and hit the ground running because you are willing to do the "What If" in order to grow? I know you are thinking "What if I fail," but I say to you, what if you fly? It is ok to be nervous because change can be scary and beautiful at the same time!

Start the day with your own personal mantra that hits home to you and is dear to your heart, and repeat it throughout the day. A **personal mantra** is an affirmation or even a scripture to help motivate and inspire you to be **your** best self. It is typically a positive phrase or statement that you use to affirm the way you want to live **your** life. Its purpose is to provide motivation and encouragement to you when you need to focus **your** mind to achieve a goal.

My personal mantra is: "My God is giving me continuous miracles and inspiring events all day long. I will meet new people and have amazing experiences that will change my life forever. I will look at everyone with an open heart, and I will connect on a deeper level to make them comfortable and want to share their 'what-if's' with me as well."

What if on this day you learned a new skill, did a good deed, tried something new or faced a fear? It just takes one step forward, and the next thing you know you will have walked through your fear.

Find the light inside you and **be the fierce woman you were meant to be.** Strong women are not born; they are forged through the fires of their challenges, hurts and mistakes.

Try this for one day and journal your results. Something tells me you might be surprised!

"There is enough fire inside you to put all of hell to shame, but you are pretending to be water for someone who is afraid to handle the dragons in your belly. Stop crushing the thing that makes you. Embrace the flames. Be whole again for yourself and no one else."

–Nikita Gill

Gill, Nikita. "The Fire Inside You". QuoteCatalog.com. Brooklyn, New York The Thought & Expression Company, 2020;
www.quotecatalog.com/quote/nikita-gill-there-is-enough-P7vkeOp
www.meanwhilepoetry.tumblr.com/

Introduction

"Be the fierce women you were meant to be!"

So, you say you are not a fierce woman; I beg to differ! Deep down inside all of us is a fierceness, a strong woman, a gladiator that fights battles we thought we could never get through!

We are way stronger than we think, beautiful on the inside even though we are so hard on our outside, givers to everyone in our lives leaving ourselves for last, smart, brave, and courageous. When life calls for courage, we are willing to muster all our strength to fight for the people we love and the life we want to live!

I bet if I sat down with any one of you ladies reading this book and told you about the circumstances you were going to endure in this life and then overcome, you would tell me there is no way you could withstand it. That is what makes us such amazing and strong women, because we can not only overcome those obstacles and hard times, but we can also learn to grow stronger and smarter and become the fierce women we are today!

I do not care what your social economic status is, where you were born, who you were born to, how much love you were given, the color of your skin, or your educational background. The fact of the matter is we all share something in common: our "story." You may think you're the only one who has gone through hard times or who has lived through something horrible, and that there's no healing from it. I guarantee you that while you think you're the only one who has lived through your story, there is always another woman who has lived through the same experience, or even a worse experience. We all have our stories, but the great news is that we can rewrite our story at any time! We can learn from others the value of that experience and take those lessons and apply them in our lives to grow, develop and march on!

In my profession as a day spa owner, I get the privilege of meeting beautiful women every day. I also get the privilege of listening and giving advice to these women, as well as receiving great advice. What I have learned over the years from these women is that what you first see when you meet them is way different from who they really are. I have come to learn that these positive, dynamic, energetic and beautiful women—inside and out—have been through horrendous circumstances. These circumstances have made them learn and grow to become the beautiful, strong and fierce women they are today.

Not only have I learned from my clients, but I have also learned life lessons through family and friends. My husband and I recently started an Italian leather handbag company called the "Natty Girl Company," where we named each Italian handbag after an inspiring woman in our lives. We had them write a mantra that they live by and a small paragraph explaining that mantra. We were blown away by the responses that we received from these ladies. They shared with us some of their most personal life experiences and struggles, which we had no idea about. You would have thought they had the most perfect lives because of their positive, glowing and radiant personalities that always shine so brightly! These ladies have become my mentors, my teachers and my strength in facing my own challenges in life.

By sharing these devotionals, my hope for you is to form a connection with another lady's experience that might help you through your own life struggles. We are not alone; we have a sisterhood of fierce women that we can connect to, learn from and grow with. Each week of the devotional is written by a different woman sharing her life experience and how she overcame her struggles to be the fierce woman she is today!

After each devotional, you will have a space to reflect and write down your challenges and fears, and how you can choose to change your mindset and rewrite your story!

My wish for you is to bring your inner light and your God-given talent out for all the world to see. It would be such a shame to leave this Earth not letting your special gift shine through.

Love to all and may you **"Be the fierce woman you were meant to be!"**

How to Use This Devotional

The fierce women devotional is divided into fifty-two weeks, with each week's devotional written by a different, inspiring, motivating and beautiful woman. These women are mothers, daughters, wives, entrepreneurs, students and caregivers. They are fierce women with good hearts that are soft but strong. They hold each other up in the storms, laugh and cry together, and, most importantly, when knocked down, they get up stronger and wiser than before!

Certain devotionals will hit home and be close to your heart because of experiences in your own life. My wish is that you may gain a little insight from each and every devotional.

After each devotional, you will be asked how this particular devotion may have affected you in some way in your life at some point in time. The devotional will make you think about how you may have responded in the past while also giving you the opportunity to see the insight through a new lens and with a different vision.

Each week you will ponder on that devotion and how it may apply to your own life. Then you will write your thoughts in the corresponding workbook area.

I encourage you, while on this journey, to envision your life in a new way by releasing old habits and taking one step in faith through all your fears to become the best version of yourself!

Week 1

Sometimes to face your fear, you have to take one small step forward in faith. That will lead to the next step, and before you know it, you will have walked through your fear.

All my life I have felt as if God was calling me to become someone great. To bring forth that special gift he planted deep inside of me a long time ago when he created me. Not that I'm anyone particularly special, because I feel that he has put that special gift inside all of us! It's our job here on earth to bring forth that gift, that light, that special talent for all to see.

I was born in the month of May with the zodiac sign of a Taurus, which makes me a bull. I would have to say I am very much like the bull; very stubborn in nature and not liking change. The thought of change scares me to death but being stagnant scares me more! The thought of never trying a new adventure, even though it could fail, scares me more than being complacent and safe.

So many times I came to those crossroads in life and had to make the tough decision on which way to go... the easy road, or the hard road where everything looks dark and scary and where there is no promise that anything could work out.

When I get on this path, I know I must rely on my faith to make the right decision, or my fear will take over. It's funny how all the "what-if's" start popping up in your mind, and before you know it, you're on a one-way train ride to self-sabotage!

So, I choose to get off that train and fly by faith! I let God take the steering wheel, and I hop into the backseat. Is it scary? Hell yes! And do I always succeed? No, but I always learn a lesson from it, and that keeps pushing me to the next level of where I am supposed to be! It's all about the journey, and I truly believe if we keep moving forward, guided by that spark that God puts in us, then eventually we'll get there!

I have not arrived yet, but I do feel a spark in my heart to help other women rise up and bring forth their light for the world to see. My hope in writing this devotional is that you will connect with one of these ladies' devotionals and that it will help you to choose the right path, knowing you're not alone in your journey!

So go forth my friend, and turn your inner spark into a full-blown fire, and **be the fierce woman you were meant to be!**

–Natalie Blake

Name 5 forks in the road where you had to choose the easy path or the hard one.

1.
2.
3.
4.
5.

Name which path you chose and how it made you feel.

____

____

____

____

____

Week 2

Live a little

Women are amazing. It's not until I had my daughter that I really knew how amazing we are.

We go through SO much. Mentally and physically. It is so hard, yet so rewarding at the same time.

We are all so alike in so many ways. We go through a lot of the same situations but struggle alone with changes in life, heartbreaks, losing weight, gaining weight, always trying to change our looks, or trying to be the perfect woman or mom.

Yet, as women, we can be so cruel to each other, and it shouldn't be like that. Be a girl's girl!! Be nice! Smile at each other, compliment! Don't judge, don't talk about each other, don't try to belittle and make someone feel less about themselves, don't talk behind backs, if you don't have something nice to say, don't say it, and don't say anything about someone's looks or size unless you are telling them how AMAZING they look! We've all been there, and it's hard! We don't need to make it harder on each other... we should be one!

Life is so short! Do what you want, when you want, how you want! Live a little! Be a good person!! Be positive!!!!! You can turn any bad situation into a positive thing. Whenever I thought my life was crashing down, that is when I would rise up stronger than ever. I look at it as a blessing and am thankful it happened, even though in that moment it never seems like one. I always remember looking back on my life when I thought something bad happened and realized it was always just opening up a door for something better that was about to come into my life, whether a job, relationship, or anything! There is always something better on its way in! Trust the journey, and the timing. It's all getting worked out for everything that you want in life to come your way, right when it's supposed to! So, stay positive and make sure you are only thinking about the things you genuinely want! Not what you don't want. Stay positive!

> *"Your life is in your hands. No matter where you are now, no matter what has happened in your life, you can begin to consciously choose your thoughts and you can change your life. There is no such thing as a hopeless situation. Every single circumstance of your life can change."*
>
> ***–Byrne, Rhonda. "The Secret." New York: Hillsboro, Oregon: Atria Books, 2006.***

Don't overthink, what you think about you bring about, stay positive and be HAPPY. Enjoy wine if you like it, eat what you want, work out... it's all about balance. Laugh, travel, and be spontaneous! When bad shit happens, it's a blessing in disguise and it makes you stronger. Always remember, karma is a bitch!

–Monica Edwards

Name 5 ways you can help build up your family, friends, coworkers or complete strangers.

1.
2.
3.
4.
5.

Describe how you felt when you were built up by a fellow woman.

WEEK 3

"Success is not final, failure is not fatal: it is the courage to continue that counts."

–Churchill, Winston. "Winston Churchill Quotes." BrainyQuote.com. BrainyMedia Inc, 2020. www.brainyquote.com/quotes/winston churchill 124653

Life seldom turns out exactly as planned. There will be ups and most certainly downs... relationships, work, etc. Often, we look at life situations as failures. Many times, these areas in our lives we deem as failures are made public. They can sometimes cause feelings of shame, embarrassment or even a loss of self-confidence.

Remember though, one event does not define you. Reframe it. Focus on what went right, what you learned from it, but most importantly, remember to believe in yourself. A strong self-belief is the key to life's endless possibilities. Dig deep. Find your courage. Persevere. The world is yours!

–Christine

Name 5 beliefs that you have held about yourself that you think define you and have made you feel bad.

1.
2.
3.
4.
5.

Name 5 ways you could reframe those beliefs, focus on your lesson from them and thank the universe for showing you!

1.
2.
3.
4.
5.

WEEK 4

"Walk with the wise and become wise; for a companion of fools suffers harm."

–Proverbs 13:20(NIV)

As a child, I was loved and led by those who wanted me to grow up faithful, healthy, strong and educated. As I grew, I still remember some of their key teachings:

- *Have you cleaned your room?*
- *Is your homework done?*
- *What have you done for your country today?*
- *If you don't have something good to say, don't say anything.*
- *Be careful who your friends are.*
- *Where are you going?*
- *Do you know I love you?*
- *Are you okay?*
- *Do you need something?*
- *Do you know what you want to be?*
- *Did you say your prayers?*

As I became a young woman, I turned from those who loved me most, pursuing adventure and independence. I was convinced I no longer needed or wanted guidance. I emulated those I spent time with. If they smoked, I smoked. If they drank, I drank. If they weren't working, I skipped work. If cheating would suffice, I cheated. I avoided those who had taught me as a child because I knew I would feel shame. I knew if they asked me a question, I would lie to them. I would give the answer they wanted. I would give the answer that made me look good, not the truth, which I knew would disappoint them.

My life began to spiral deeper and deeper into despair and disappointment. I found myself a young, divorced, single mother, no longer surrounded by people who truly loved me. I was disconnected from my faith. I was bankrupt financially and spiritually. I prayed to God asking him why He was punishing me. Why had He let me get into this situation? Didn't He love me?

Left with little, I turned back to those who loved me. I asked for help. My parents and grandparents babysat so I could work a legitimate job. I was encouraged by my friends at work to go back to school. I was told how I could qualify for a low-income home. A generous, loving man entered my life.

Today, I continue to start each day with God. I take a close look at how I am spending my days. I look closely at those around me, and I find we share these things in common:

- *We are on a personal journey with God.*
- *We are part of a supportive church community.*
- *We donate time and resources to help others.*
- *We make family a priority.*
- *We believe in education.*
- *We show up for work ready to do our best.*
- *We eat, sleep and exercise.*
- *We keep our home in order.*
- *We save money wisely.*
- *We are willing to sacrifice "wants" in order to provide for "needs."*

I can tell you from my experience, Proverbs 13:20 is my daily truth. When I'm around God-led, hard-working, positive people, I learn to be God-led, hard-working and positive. Choose those around you well!

–Theresa Johnson

Name 5 events in your life when you turned away from your faith, family and friends.

1.
2.
3.
4.
5.

When you turned back to your faith, family and friends, how did your life turn around?

Week 5

Find the Extraordinary in the Ordinary - Every Day

I know, this phrase doesn't seem the least bit fierce or courageous. However, I have found that it is the most powerfully positive mantra you can have.

When I first began writing this article, the world was normal. I got up every day and went to work. My children went to school, and we all planned and stressed and lived among each other. Once the coronavirus (2020) moved in, the trajectory of each of our lives changed, and priorities shifted in relation. The mantra that I live by suddenly took on more importance.

I am a lawyer who works with children and families that are in crisis. Many of the people whom I deal with on a daily basis have addictions to drugs, have been affected by domestic violence or are homeless and unable to care properly for themselves or their families. Their lives are chaotic and unpredictable. Each day brings a new set of challenges that they rarely have the capability to negotiate. Their children are placed in situations that are often transitory. Many times, they jump from placement to placement, barely staying long enough to learn the names of those who care for them. For them, every day is a day of real chaos and confusion.

Working with people in these situations has made me pause. Sometimes when we live our lives surrounded by plenty, we forget what "wanting" is. Instead of appreciating what we have, we focus on the "more" that we see in others and we covet their lives. We often lose sight of all the good things we possess and the beauty of what surrounds us. We fail to recognize the extraordinary occurrences that happen to us each and every day. Things like being able to kiss our children good morning and good night. Having the ability and the means to house and feed the people who need us, not to mention provide for their comfort and entertainment. The basic blessing of having someone in our lives who cares enough to want to know how we are. Being conscious of the realities of others may cause the burdens of our everyday to take on a different appearance.

A number of years ago my uncle got and eventually died from a glioblastoma tumor in his brain. We watched him struggle with the daily loss of his ability to function normally. One of the most notable losses for him was his ability to laugh. My interactions and memories of him from my childhood were filled with laughter, and the absence of it was unsettling. Occasionally, his brain would rally, and he would chuckle at something he heard. Under normal circumstances, likely no one would have noticed the sound. But in the relative silence, the small noise was extraordinary.

Retrain yourself to look for the special parts of the life that you already know. See the fortune that surrounds you each day, and find something extraordinary in the regular rhythm of life.

> *"There are so many things you can learn about, but you'll miss the best things if you keep your eyes shut."*
>
> ***–Seuss, Dr. "I Can Read With My Eyes Shut!" New York: Beginner Books, 1978.***

–Allison Owen

Name 5 things you are grateful for that you may have taken for granted in your life.

1.
2.
3.
4.
5.

Name 5 ways you can retrain your mind to be more appreciate of these gifts and blessings you are given in life.

1.
2.
3.
4.
5.

Week 6

In my world everyone is holding hands, drinking their favorite beverages, and singing "We are the World." I say cherish all the small things in life.

Starting from humble beginnings, I have always had to work hard for everything I own. I have grown to appreciate all the small things in life and realized simplicity is the way to go. Truly in gratitude, I am blessed for all my accomplishments and "heart-ships." They have made me the person I am today. I want to be remembered for having the biggest heart and compassion for all people, making a difference in their lives.

In my twenties I strived to have my own business. I worked on my days off, trying to make and save all that I could. I went through many transitions in the process, all of which have served me well. In my thirties I got caught up in the rat race. I lost myself for a minute, and time flew by. All I wanted was to be successful and feel fulfilled. In my forties I realized that most of my time was spent working. I was missing balance and boundaries. I made a decision that from then on out I would make time for family, friends and me. I would minimize clutter, find self-peace, and put what is important to me before work.

There has to be a balance. At this point in my life, I am on the right track. I take nothing for granted, and I have faith that I will have everything I need in life because I am positive, simple, and, most of all, content with where I am in life. I will always be grateful for life lessons. They have brought me to where I am today. This is who I am and where I am going....

–Denise Ann Warner

When you have placed money, material objects or yourself first at the cost of others, how did it make you feel?

When you have learned to live simply, appreciate the small things, and give thanks for your blessings, how did you feel?

Week 7

Life is short.... So get on with it.

"In this way, love has been perfected among us, so that we may have confidence on the day of judgment; for in this world we are just like Him."

1 John 4:17(NIV)

I was blessed with knowing exactly what I wanted to do with my life when I grew up. I always wanted to be a singer with my favorite singers being South Africa's Brenda Fassie and Sweden's ABBA. From the moment I could remember, my dreams were set and sure. I would sing. As a youngster I did not think about singing "for the Lord." I just wanted to share what I knew God had given me: a voice.

But as I grew into my teens and then young adulthood, I realized the world was filled with singers, many singers, and many who were more accomplished and diligent and more equipped than I was. Why would anyone want to listen to me if they could hear Whitney Houston or others like her? So slowly I laid down my goals and tools and occasionally sang in the safety of a church worship team. At least I was singing. It wasn't half the size of my dream or my "calling," but it was something. Until tragedy hit and my son passed away at twenty months old, and I was quickly and sadly reminded that not all of us will live to be seventy-five. Some of us only have five years, some forty, to accomplish what we have been placed on this earth for and, more importantly, what we have been saved for. God has a "special" and unique plan for each and every one of us. I did not one day want to stand before Him and when asked, "What I had done with my gift?" and not be able to answer that I had lived my best life. Instead giving "reasons" like "Well I was busy studying, or having a family," or "Whitney Houston was so much better than me at singing." I want to hear God say, "Well done my good and faithful servant...." because I have taken his given talent and worked it and polished it and multiplied it, for His Glory. I don't know how much time I have to fulfill His plan for my life... so every day I will show up as God intended for me. Living, listening, dreaming, fulfilling His unique plan. Go on, get on with it.

Ecclesiastes 3:2(NIV) *"A time to be born and a time to die, a time to plant and a time to uproot."*

2 Corinthians 5:10(NIV) *"For we must all appear before the judgment seat of Christ, that each one may receive his due for the things done in the body, whether good or bad."*

–Audrey Mbuyazi

Today is as good a day as any day to start living your God-given dreams. What are they?

____

____

____

Dreams need support, so who shall you ask to run this race with you?

____

____

____

Week 8

"Done is better than perfect"

–Sandberg, Sheryl., and Nell Scovell. "Lean In: Women, Work, and the Will to Lead." First edition. New York: Alfred A. Knopf, 2013.

I've battled my whole life with perfection. I used to think that in order to be worthy, I had to be perfect. That's a tall order. And it left me wondering, "Will I ever be good enough?"

Smart enough, skinny enough, pretty enough, courageous enough... I never felt like anything I did was ever enough. It left me ragged—so tied up in perfection, comparison and guilt. My negative inner dialogue was on a constant loop. Maybe you've been there too?

It kept me from living. And I'm not being dramatic. Chasing perfection was paralyzing because I was so afraid to fail. But eventually I realized the exhaustion wasn't worth it. I realized the reason people loved me had nothing to do with how "perfect" I was or wasn't. I realized that as an adult, there's no one to give you a gold star or an "A." I realized that allowing fear or procrastination to take over didn't help me at all; in fact, it kept me from doing the things I really cared about and the things I really wanted to do.

And so, I adopted this mantra—that done is better than perfect. Because it's easier to agonize over everything, including this note to you. If I sit here for hours, taking apart every word, until I feel like it's "perfect," two things can happen. First, maybe I finally feel like it's "worthy," but I've wasted so much of my time that I can't do the other things I wanted to do. Or worse, I might feel that this is and will never be perfect, so I never send it off to you.

There's one thing I know for certain—it's that we all have unique gifts to share with the world, that we NEED to share with the world. And so we can't get caught up in whether or not they're perfect. Instead we need your gifts to be out there; we need you to be out there.

Choosing that "done is better than perfect" has had a huge impact on my life. It has helped me keep moving even when I was afraid or feeling stuck. It helped me when I was laid off from my job—from writing my resume to applying for jobs and interviewing. It helped me start my own career and life coaching practice: helping perfectionists quiet their negative self-talk too.

Because done doesn't mean sloppy, I still do my best. Instead I let go of chasing perfection because that just isn't attainable.

–Liesl Drought

Name 5 events, tasks, or dreams that you have wanted to try but have put on hold because you felt that you had to be perfect first.

1.
2.
3.
4.
5.

Name 5 outcomes that may happen if you choose to move forward in faith anyway without being perfect.

1.
2.

3.
4.
5.

Week 9

Stop Capitalizing Your I

Once when working at a camp, I asked God to give me a goal for the week. The first thought that popped into my mind was to be humble, and I thought, "Who, me? I take pride in my humbleness!" But when I stopped to think, I realized that every day consisted of me complaining about how hard the work was.

In the English language, we capitalize the words "God" and "I," but not the word "you." It is as if our language sets us up to think of ourselves as equals with God and to think of others as less important than ourselves. In Philippians 2:5-8 Paul writes, "Let this mind be in you which was also in Christ Jesus: Who, existing in the form of God, did not consider equality with God something to be grasped, but emptied Himself, taking the form of a servant, being made in human likeness. And being found in appearance as a man, He humbled Himself and became obedient to death—even death on a cross."

Jesus was the son of God but did not come to Earth to flaunt His heavenly position. Instead He took the position of a servant and willingly died a painful, humiliating death so we can have eternal life. He laid down His life for you and me. When we focus on ourselves, we do the Kingdom of God a disservice. We make our presence known instead of the Holy Spirit.

I'm not saying we should avoid being real with God and those around us about what we are going through. Be real! But think about others too.

If your roommate forgets to do the dishes, why not be a servant and wash them yourself? Look at Jesus. He even washed Judas's feet (John 13). When people at work irritate you, instead of complaining, pray for them. Lastly, draw two circles on your hands. When you complain, look down at your hands. Remember what Jesus did for you, as your daily complaints are probably not as bad as what He has gone through for you.

–Natalya DiCiacca

Name 5 complaints you say often that are really not that bad compared to other people's problems.

1.
2.
3.
4.
5.

Name 5 ways you can take those complaints and turn them around to help serve others or yourself in a more positive light.

1.
2.
3.
4.
5.

Week 10

"I can do all things through Christ who strengthens me."

Philippians 4:13(KJV)

I am truly fortunate to have come from a loving family with eight brothers and sisters, and parents that lived their faith daily. I know this is how God prepared me for the work I now do. After being a nurse for twenty-three years, I became a forensic nurse, and this changed the course of my career.

Going through graduate school, working full time, on-call as a forensic nurse with three children and a supportive husband, life was pretty crazy. I am a strong "C" student but received "A's" in every class! This was proof enough that Christ was in charge, He had a plan for me and I just needed to let Him lead.

I used to have a phobia about speaking in public. Yet, as a forensic nurse, I had to testify in court, and I was asked to do public speaking. Just the thought of speaking in front of people would make me break out in a cold sweat. It took time, but when I realized how important it was to educate healthcare workers on how to care for those experiencing violence, I was able to put my fears aside, knowing my strength did not come from me, it came from Christ. That is empowering.

Now I love training healthcare and legal professionals on the community response to violence, including those exploited through trafficking. When I look back, I am amazed at the transformation, knowing the strength and fierceness that comes from Christ who is working through me. Pretty cool.

There is a song by Chris Tomlin that says,

> *"Whom shall, I fear / I know Who goes before me / I know Who stands behind / The God of angel armies / is always on my side / The One who reigns forever/ He is a Friend of mine."*

> ***–Tomlin, Chris. "Whom Shall I Fear [God of Angel Armies]". Burning Lights. United States, 2012***

Philippians 4 6-7(NIV) *"Do not be anxious about anything, but in every situation, by prayer and petition, with thanksgiving, present your requests to God. And the peace of God, which transcends all understanding, will guard your hearts and your minds in Christ Jesus."*

–Ruth Downing

Name 5 fears you know you could not have walked through without a higher power.

1.
2.
3.
4.
5.

What were the results when you faced your fears by trusting your higher power?

____

____

____

Week 11

Never be too busy to enjoy the small things. Sometimes the smallest things mean the most.

In this busy and changing world, I try to slow down to enjoy the small moments, because sometimes they mean the most. It can be as simple as taking the time to hold my daughter in the middle of cleaning or making dinner. I will look down and see these tiny hands reaching up or pulling my hand towards her, signaling for me to sit with her. It can be so easy to be consumed with what I am doing, but these moments mean so much. I know in the blink of an eye my girls will no longer be looking for me to hold them.

Becoming a mother at a young age has played a big part in shaping my life. At such a young age I was faced with very real obstacles. Overcoming those hurdles and moving forward has gotten me to where I am now. I have learned to appreciate the small moments in life. I've been blessed with a very loving and supportive family. I strive to do the same for my children by giving them the love and support they need to succeed in life.

Pulling away from the hustle and bustle of life to be present in my children's' life is especially important to me. At times I feel like I am failing and there just simply is not enough of me to go around. But then one of my girls will unexpectedly tell me they love me or tell me I am the best mom. And although there's always opportunity for improvement, that is all I need to keep moving forward. At this point in my life, the best advice I could give someone is to slow down and really enjoy the moments in life that are so important. Life on earth is far too short; enjoy every moment, big and small.

–Amanda Francis

Name 5 small moments you wish you would have slowed down and enjoyed.

1.
2.
3.
4.
5.

Name 5 events in your life now, that you can stop and enjoy, so they will be memories you will cherish forever.

1.
2.
3.
4.
5.

Week 12

A good deed every day is good for the soul... more than one and your cup will runneth over!

This became something that I do daily, after a stranger truly touched my heart.

We had two girls under the age of two. My husband was working full time and going to school full time. We had recently moved. I had my own business: a hair salon with eleven employees. I was a working stylist too.

I was "still" mourning the miscarriage of twins (three years prior). I was angry that our fertility treatments cost so much money. Really.... I was just so tired!

The girls were a little fussy that morning, and it was starting to snow. The news said a big storm was coming. It was my day off; my usual shopping day. I had to go to the store, so I bundled everyone up, and away we went. By the time I pulled into the parking lot, the snow had already fallen a couple of inches. The store was very busy for 8:00 a.m. on a Monday! I went through the store as quickly as I could, with one in a car seat carrier and the other strapped onto me with a kangaroo-type carrier. Forty-five minutes later, I'm in the checkout line.

As I start to take the groceries out of the cart, both of my girls start crying. They aren't hungry. They aren't wet. I put a few more items on the conveyor belt and apologize to the cashier, who is giving me "the look" (like can't you make a three-month-old and a twenty-month-old stop crying!?). I think to myself, "What's wrong? I hope they aren't getting sick." And then it happens. Yep! You guessed it; one threw up. Then

I start to cry. People are staring at me. I'm scrambling for wipes. I am cleaning up puke, and I feel a soft touch on my shoulder.

I turn to see an older woman with a gentle smile. I was afraid it was going to be the man who was not at all happy that he was in line behind me. He had gone to another line, away from my "hot mess"! The smiling woman said, "This too shall pass... In the meantime, may I please help you so that you and your beautiful babies can get home before it gets much worse out?" I don't even think I answered her, but she was unloading my cart for me while I finished cleaning up. She made small talk the entire time. I got us all bundled up and paid. I thanked her... Ok, actually I hugged her!! I am thankful for her and the "good deed" she did for me on that winter day twenty years ago.

There are angels amongst us. This is my "WHY," why I try to do a Daily Good Deed. Trust me... it is good for the soul!

–Christine

List five events in your life that made you feel special through the help of a stranger.

1.
2.
3.
4.
5.

List five events when you helped a stranger and how it made you feel.

1.
2.
3.

4.
5.

WEEK 13

"The longer I live, the more I realize the impact of attitude on life. Attitude, to me, is more important than education, than money, than circumstances, than failures, than success, than what other people think or say or do. It is more important than appearance, giftedness or skill. It will make or break a company...church.... a home. The remarkable thing is we have a choice everyday regarding the attitude we embrace for that day. We cannot change our past...we cannot change the fact that people act in a certain way. We cannot change the inevitable. The only thing we can do is play on the one string we have, and that is our attitude... I am convinced that life is 10% what happens to me and 90% how I react to it. And so, it is with you...we are in charge of our ATTITUDES."

By Chuck Swindoll
–Swindoll, Charles. "Charles R. Swindoll Quotes." Quotes.net. STANDS4 LLC, 2020
www.quotes.net/quote/17859

In my life I have had many challenges. Some were a result of poor decisions, and some were a result of just living. Sometimes life just came at me from all sides. You know how it is. Sometimes it just seems like everything is wrong and nothing is right. It's like the whole world is against you, and you are swimming upstream in a river that is very deep and has a lot of rapids. You just feel like you are drowning. The details of my life are not all that important. Let me just say that Paul the Apostle never disclosed in scripture what his "thorn in the flesh" was. I think that was on purpose so that we don't think it applied to that situation alone. We all have a thorn in the flesh. How we respond to it makes all the difference in the world. Paul says it best in Philippians 4:8-9: "And now, dear brothers and sisters, one final thing. Fix your thoughts on what is true, and honorable, and right, and pure, and lovely and admirable. Think about things that are excellent and worthy of praise. Keep putting into practice all you learned and received from me – everything you heard from me and saw me doing. Then the God of peace will be with you" (Philippians 4:8-9 NLT).

Whatever you are going through, practice thinking good thoughts. Keep a good attitude. You are not in this alone. The God of Peace will comfort you.

–Deborah Pintz

Name 5 thorns in your side that you have reacted to negatively and how each made you feel.

1.
2.
3.
4.
5.

Name 5 positive attitudes you could develop towards these thorns and the possible outcomes that could follow.

1.
2.
3.
4.
5.

WEEK 14

"I've learned that people will forget what you said, people will forget what you did, but people will never forget how you made them feel."

–Angelou, Maya. "Maya Angelou Quotes." BrainyQuote.com. BrainyMedia Inc, 2020. www.brainyquote.com/quotes/maya_angelou_392897

I was raised to be an independent woman, always encouraged to think for myself, make my own choices and pave my own way. From a young age, I was expected to go to college and use my mind to make an impact. At the same time, I knew I wanted to do something to help people and make a difference, which is what motivated me to become a nurse practitioner.

Now, there are some dates in my life that I will clearly never forget: my high school and college graduations, my wedding date, the days I brought my children into this world, September 11, 2001, and March 24, 2020—the day the Governor of Indiana declared the "stay at home" order due to the coronavirus. In all my years of practicing in healthcare, I have never seen anything like this, as I know no one else has. I watched as my kids were given one day to clean out their lockers for what they thought would be a three-week break from school. I have observed the fear and panic escalate rapidly in the general public due to the unknown. And then, I have also witnessed the selflessness and courage of my healthcare family.

In such uncertain and frightening times, it can be difficult to be optimistic. As I have adjusted to my new norm, I still try to look for the positive. But if I'm really being honest, most days I struggle with a mixture of apprehension and obligation. Fortunately, I am surrounded by peers who encourage and inspire me to push through. This is, after all, why I went into the medical field in the first place—to care for those most vulnerable and give them a sense of hope. So even with all the challenges we are facing right now during this pandemic, I wouldn't want to be doing anything else.

Despite so much sadness, I have also seen an abundance of joy and gratitude. The feeling of coming home after a long, exhausting day and finding a "hero" sign in my yard is beyond humbling; it motivates me to do better and be better. Ultimately, I am attempting to be an example for my own daughter, showing her that you can be a strong woman while simultaneously being a caring human being. I think that is the true beauty of women in our modern day: we can be and do all!

–Kelly Prather

Name defining moments in your life that changed you forever.

____

____

____

____

____

Name the gifts or life lessons from those experiences that you can pass on to others.

____

____

____

____

Week 15

"I am the true vine, and My Father is the vinedresser. Every branch in Me that does not bear fruit He takes away; and every branch that bears fruit He prunes, that it may bear more fruit."

John 15: 1-2(NKJV)

There's one thing about living in a wine growing region; the words of Jesus about being the true vine, and his subsequent teachings, all spring vividly to life. From the leafy abundance of the vines weighing down the trellis above my friend's terrace to the neatly trimmed rows descending the slopes in their flaming autumn colors as the harvest approaches, I can picture it all so clearly. These days, pruning is mostly mechanized. In Jesus's time it was an endless, back-breaking chore for the vinedresser, as vines grow at a phenomenal rate. Contrast that abundance with the bare vines in winter. Here, pruning remains a manual task to this day. Each branch must be cut back with ruthless precision until all that remain are two, or at most three, thin, hard-trimmed branches sticking out from the gnarled stock. They are then securely tied to supporting wires to wait for the return of spring. All the rest is thrown out.

What does this have to do with us; with me?

God prunes us in a number of ways, and the process is rarely without pain. Even if, under the Holy Spirit's conviction, we are willing to lay down some cherished personal project or position, there will still be a sense of loss.

Jesus says, “If you love me, you will obey my commands” (John 14:15). We say: “Yes, Lord, I love you, but...” So, we hang on too long because we also love what we do: the admiration of others; the glory of our giftedness; the satisfaction of serving. Then the Lord allows a different sort of pruning. The sharp shears of jealousy or rejection arrive to cut us down to size. We may lose a job, a promotion or a friendship. That hurts.

Finally, we may face illness. For a while we struggle to carry on until we eventually admit, with a greater or lesser amount of grace, that we have to stop. We lay down our ambition or our reputation. Remember, though, as we lose our life, we gain His. When Jesus truly is our all in all, we can at last be still and know that He is God; our God. We know Him and are fully known by Him. What joy.

Without fear, we can embrace the cross for the joy that is set before us: our resurrection life with Him.

–Sarah Cunnington

Name 5 events in your life that you need to let God prune, but you keep holding onto that dead vine.

1.
2.
3.
4.
5.

Name 5 ways you could choose to let go of trying to control each of these events and let God do the necessary pruning.

1.
2.

3.
4.
5.

WEEK 16

"I am enough. I have enough. I've done enough."

–C., Diane. "I Am Enough, I Have Enough, I Do Enough". Medium.com, 2019 www.medium.com/know-thyself-heal-thyself/i-am-enough-i-have-enough-i-do-enough-10774ec9f776

One of the joys and privileges of my job as a life coach is having deep, intimate conversations with extraordinary women who courageously open up and reveal their hearts to me. The most common theme of those conversations is our fear of not being enough.

Not pretty enough, thin enough, smart enough, organized enough...

You name it and we are not enough of it.

This is a feeling we all wrestle with. Our deepest fear is that we aren't worthy enough to be loved. So let's settle this once and for all.

Being enough is not a real thing.

Really.

If it were, who decides that we are enough? Where is the dividing line of enough/not enough? Is a baby enough? At what age does that baby become not enough, and why?

And yet, we all FEEL unworthy at times. Why? Because every one of us has a brain that tells us we are. It is the job of our very well-intentioned but somewhat misguided brain to protect us.

Each and every one of us has a brain that is hard-wired to tell us we are not enough in order to prevent us from doing anything it considers risky, hard or just plain uncomfortable.

Our job is to simply understand how our brain works and then lovingly supervise it.

THE QUESTION HAS ALREADY BEEN ANSWERED.

We each have inherent value, simply because we are alive. We were created to live and to love, and to do it in our own unique way.

CHOOSE to believe it. FEEL your worthiness.

DECIDE to never entertain the question of your worthiness again.

DECIDE to love your life, your body, your job right now.

DECIDE to take the energy you spent feeling bad about yourself and spend it on creating the life YOU ARE WORTHY of.

Consider this your personal invitation to create and to live the life of your dreams. All it takes is a decision.

–Marcy Kocher

Name 5 areas in your life where you feel like you are not enough.

1.
2.
3.
4.
5.

Name 5 different ways you can look at these areas of your life and choose to believe you are enough right now, and choose to love yourself the way you are.

1.
2.
3.

4.
5.

Week 17

Say Yes!

When I was young, up until I started high school, I said yes to everything that sounded at all interesting to me. 4-H, baseball, dance classes, soccer, cheerleading, band, newspaper, and on and on. If I had a bad experience with an activity, or found it just wasn't my thing, I simply didn't sign up to continue. Then something happened. Something in me changed. I'd receive information about an activity or event, and even if my first reaction was excitement or interest, I'd pull back and think about all the reasons not to do it. "Well, so-and-so already does that and is way better than I am." Or, "What if I try and fail? I'll be humiliated." So pretty much through high school, until my mid-thirties, that's how I lived—only doing things I knew I could do well. Do you see the problem with that?! Where's the growth? How do you learn anything if you only do what you already do well?

So, what changed in my mid-thirties? I was a stay-at-home mom of two very energetic boys, and my husband was killing it with his business, which meant it was usually just me and the boys all day. I loved the privilege of being home with the kids, nurturing them and helping them grow physically and mentally strong, but I knew I needed to do the same for myself. I started by saying yes to fitness classes at our local YMCA, which led to signing up for classes of interest at the community college one night a week. A couple years later I got a part-time job... a job I said yes to only because a friend asked me to interview, not because I was confident in my abilities.

It sounded like fun to work with my friend, make some new friends and challenge myself. I started thinking about what could go right instead of what could go wrong. I found that the more I was saying yes based on my gut reaction instead of overthinking it, the more I was growing, and the more fulfilled I was feeling.

Now I'm much more like my younger self, as far as saying yes. I trust my instinct to say yes (even when it scares me), and I know that I'll figure it out as I go. If you want to grow, you must get out of your comfort zone! You only get one life... say yes to it!!!

–*Amy Ellet Bauman*

Name opportunities you've been given that you wanted to try, but stopped yourself due to fear of the unknown. How did that make you feel?

Name opportunities you have been offered that you were afraid of, but said yes to anyway. How did that make you feel?

WEEK 18

No matter how bad things are... it's always better to look at the bright side.

Life has taught me that looking at the bright side makes it much easier to deal with the events and situations that are thrown at us. Looking at the bright side gives me hope and allows me to bring hope to others.

I have found life to be an emotional roller coaster with lots of ups and downs. It is easy to be happy and content when things are going well, but as bad things happen, life can get tough. I have found that sharing the bright side of a situation can have an amazing impact on me, personally, as well as on friends and family. Unfortunately, many people are not initially open to hearing the bright side of their issue. However, hearing the bright side can often provide them with great comfort.

Looking at the bright side enables us to take the focus off or ourselves and appreciate and give thanks for all the blessings we have in our lives. Dwelling on the bad only brings us down. Throughout my life, my nature has always been to find the good in every circumstance and think about the bright side. Many times, the "good side" is not immediately obvious, but I know it is always there. Sometimes I cannot find it right away, but I've learned that after prayer and contemplation, the bright side always appears.

My faith is the foundation that helps me focus on the good in everything and allows me to deal with the bad. One of my guiding scriptures helping me to always look at the bright side is Thessalonians 5:16-19(NIV). "Rejoice always, pray continually, give thanks in all circumstances; for this is God's will for you in Christ Jesus. Do not quench the Spirit."

Knowing God is in control of everything assures me that whatever I am dealing with has a purpose far beyond my understanding. Even failure has a bright side and helps me to learn from it and "fail forward." Looking at the bright side has proven to be a powerful tool to help me through life's challenges. Give it a try!

–Mary Jane Bowman

Name events in your life when you chose to look on the bright side instead of the negative. How did that make you feel?

____

____

____

____

____

____

Name moments when you helped someone else look on the positive side of the event. How did that make them feel?

____

____

____

____

____

____

____

Week 19

"A flower does not think of competing with the flower next to it. It just blooms!"

–Sensei Ogui. "Zen Shin Talks". Cleveland, Ohio: Zen Shin Buddhist Publications, 1998.

What speaks to me about this quote is the trap of comparison. It's something I have dealt with and have learned to be aware of when it rears its ugly head.

I love being a woman, and I have learned to love myself. It's a beautiful and freeing moment when we accept that we all have "true beauty"! That true beauty comes from the inside out. It's contagious, free, glorious, inspiring... and you have it!

Each of us has unique gifts that lead us to the best version of ourselves, if we are willing to accept, appreciate, nurture and honor those gifts. When we come to the place where we truly love and accept our unique individual gifts and choose to use them, we can serve and inspire other women to do the same. That is our genuine, authentic, and complete self, living our most purposeful, intentional life that we were created to live.

Jeremiah 29:11: "For I know the plans I have for you, plans to prosper you and not harm you, plans to give you hope and a future."

Today I am grateful to be a woman and blessed to know many women who inspire me! My desire is to love and inspire other women to look at the unique abilities they have to offer the world, rather than comparing themselves to others.

Ephesians 2:10: "For we are God's masterpiece. He has created us anew in Christ Jesus, so we can do the good things He planned for us long ago."

That's right, you are a masterpiece! I am a masterpiece!

What strengths and talents do you have? How can you merge your natural God-given abilities to live your fullest, most purposeful life? You are inspiring someone today and every day! Rise up my friend and stand tall; you are loved, special and needed in this world. Women need women to exemplify self-love and love for others!

Blessings & Joy
–Dreana Nealon

Name ways you self-sabotage by criticizing yourself, and how it makes you feel.

____

____

____

____

____

Name how you feel when you look at your faults with self-love and acceptance.

____

____

____

____

____

Week 20

"Keep a clear eye toward life's end.
Do not forget your purpose and destiny as God's child.
What you are in His sight is what you are and nothing more.
Remember that when you leave this earth, you can take nothing
that you have received –
fading symbols of honor, trappings of power –
but only what you have given:
a full heart enriched by honest service, love, sacrifice and courage."

–St Francis of Assisi as attributed by: Guillebaud, Simon. "Choose Life: 365 Readings for Radical Disciples". United Kingdom: Lion Hudson Limited, 2014.

I focus on living one day at a time—yesterday is gone (you cannot change anything that has happened) and tomorrow isn't here yet, so don't create anxiety about something that doesn't exist.

Living in day-tight compartments, focusing on love and giving, keeps me grounded. Gratitude—enumerating my blessings daily—and trust in God's plan, no matter what is happening in my life, helps keep me calm and centered.

–Beth Yaekle

How do you feel when you focus on the past or the future instead of the present moment?

How do you feel when you focus more on loving and giving of yourself and being present in the moment?

Week 21

"To thine own self be true."

–Shakespeare, William. "Hamlet". Act 1, Scene 3. 1603

This mantra is dear to me, because during my life's journey, I've had so many experiences that were negative. Experiences where people didn't like me or for whatever reason, treated me as if I didn't matter. This used to really bother me because I knew in my heart I treated people with love and respect. Even when I was treated wrong, I didn't carry that into the next relationship, but there were some people who treated me in a way that was damaging.

From the start of my adult life, I was in several abusive relationships. The first was by my husband, who is the father of my five children. I dated him for three years before we were married. I had no clue he could be abusive or that he had a temper. I lived in this reality for pretty much twelve years of my marriage. I was choked, smothered and kidnapped, and I was even part of a high-speed chase because he was running from the police with me in the car.

I suffered a lot of trauma, shame and humiliation. For years I kept it to myself, for the most part. But then I began to realize I was greater than what was happening to me. I joined support groups, received counseling and became empowered.

Many times, we live our lives based on what someone else thinks, or if they will approve of us or include us. We base the trajectory of our lives on whether people will accept us or not. But when you allow your true essence to shine bright, and operate in what you have been given to do and what speaks to your spirit, you will live to your highest and greatest self. Then I think you are really being true to who you are.

Being true to yourself requires you to be unapologetically and authentically you, in a positive regard. I don't need your approval when I'm confident in who I am. When I know my God-given purpose, others' opinions of me can't stop my progress. So, I don't base my movement on what others think. I walk the path that was given to me and affect the lives I'm meant to affect. When you do this, no one can hold you prisoner. Operate outside of the box, outside of your own box, and then get out of your own way.

Live the life you were created to live. When you do this, you'll find true freedom, and a peace no one can take from you.

–Neicy Squire

Name times in your life when you based your self-worth on someone else's opinion of you. How did that make you feel?

____

____

____

____

____

When you learn to believe in your own self-worth and not the opinions of others, how do you feel?

____

____

____

____

____

Week 22

Forgiveness is not for others but for yourself!

It is really hard to forgive someone, and even harder to forgive yourself. Forgiveness is extremely important for a person's mental health and well-being. When we have been hurt, wronged or scandalized, there is no other way to overcome, than to forgive. I am not saying to forget, but with forgiveness you can soften the pain. Forgiving others is something I am very good at doing. Forgiving myself however, is an exceptionally long and frustrating process I am still working on. Of course, there are different degrees to the pain of being hurt by someone. I get that! But to carry that burden of pain with you every day is too much for your mind and body to bear. Give that pain right back to the person who inflicted it by forgiving. You are not giving them a pass on their actions or words; you are not accepting what they have done; you are telling them you will heal from this and you will no longer be THEIR VICTIM. This is not easy, but it is for the health of yourself.

I am a firm believer that stress can kill, and by carrying your pain, you can be slowly killing yourself. When I grant forgiveness, I feel the heaviness of the pain and stress leave me. Forgiving yourself is completely different though. You are the inflictor and the victim. I am a continual work in progress on this. I dissect (and I mean dissect) all the parts leading up to and including the action that needs forgiven. By dissecting, some circumstances come to the forefront and explanations are discovered. We are human, and with that comes faults, flaws and facts.

Every day… ok, most days, I try to identify something I like about myself. Then I find something I don't like so much and forgive myself for this flaw. It does help me identify what I want to work on so I won't have to work as hard to forgive myself. Try and learn to be a forgiver. It is good for your soul!

–Sandy

Name events or people you have not forgiven, or even times when you feel you have not forgiven yourself. How does that make you feel?

Name steps you can take to help dissect the problem and move towards forgiveness.

Week 23

"Comparison is the thief of joy."
I created YOU for big things, so stay in your lane and do YOU.

–Quote attributed to Theodore Roosevelt. A to Z Quotes.
www.azquotes.com/quote/501479

My body was still asleep as my mind crept awake. Eyes still closed, I could hear the hum of the fan, and the smell of coffee filled the air. My usual mental checklist of to-dos didn't automate. I just laid there. Frozen with a weight of sadness on me like a big heavy blanket.

This isn't me. I mean, I don't jump out of bed with a smile on my face. But I do wake up focused and ready to roll for the most productive part of my day.

I laid there and prayed. I recounted the day before looking for a cause for this ho-hum feeling. I had hosted a highly skilled trainer to help my team on a call the night before.

And she was amazing! I went to bed feeling on top of the world. So why the doldrum morning?

And then it hit me: I felt inadequate.

You see, somewhere in the night, Satan got in my head. This trainer is someone I aspire to be like. She is the next level in my book. I went to bed ecstatic at the positive response from my team, but woke up feeling that because she is SO good, I am less than. It made no sense, but the feeling was real.

God showed me in that moment that comparison is the thief of joy. He gave me MY strengths and abilities, and He gave her HERS. Comparing my gifts to hers robbed me of the joy she brought to me and my team, and it took me from the top of the world to the depths of inadequacy disguised as sadness.

When that clicked, I rolled out of bed, choosing to replace inadequacy with owning the woman God created me to be. And to stay in my lane and be ME.

–Renee

Name times in your life when you compared yourself to others, and how it stole your joy.

Name strengths, abilities and gifts that have been given to you that make you unique.

Week 24

The Bible is my operational manual.

I had no idea that I was missing pieces and was never given the necessary tools. With over two decades of successful, independent operation, in a series of events over a short period, it all changed. He chose me (John 15:16)!

Recklessness and rule breaking, by nature, was all I knew. I had no idea I came from a dysfunctional family with generational curses guiding my ways. I had hurts, habits and hang-ups that were taking up all the space in my toolbox.

When God started working in me, He knew I needed a new foundation (Matthew 7:24). From rock bottom, we began this journey together. Watching sermons and studying became interesting to me. I finally understood some of the Bible! I joined a couple of Christ-centered groups, since my old environment and associates no longer felt comforting. I was changing before my eyes (Isaiah 43:19). It was during this time that God softened my heart and gave me blessings of peace and joy. It took two years, but like Jesus talks about childbirth in John 16:21-22, He gave me so much joy, I hardly recall the anguish.

What I do know is that God's Word is the truth. It is filled with stories, poetry and historical facts, all written to provide guidance in getting to know God, finding freedom through integrity and discovering that we are here for a purpose.

God loves all of us so much. He is excited to have a relationship with us. He promises that if we trust in Jesus, our burden will be light (Matthew 11:30). Yes, we will face troubles (John 16:33), but when we trust, even when we don't understand His ways (Proverbs 3:5), and use Paul's epistles as our FAQ reference, our relationship with God and receipt of His power is life changing. Before your eyes, all your pieces and parts will be functioning and fully operational for eternity.

–Melissa Vergiels

Name 5 items in your toolbox that have not been serving your greater good.

1.
2.
3.
4.
5.

Name 5 tools from God's word that you could use to replace these dysfunctional tools.

1.
2.
3.
4.
5.

Week 25

GOD: FOR me and THROUGH me

More importantly than ever, we need this truth: God is first FOR me, then He works THROUGH me.

We women often function as multidimensional servants. We serve our families, our employers, our churches, our communities, and even God's Kingdom. Too often we give of ourselves to depletion because we fail to properly position ourselves to receive the source (God's love), before we give the supply (God's love).

As His servant, I must constantly remind myself of this truth: God's heart is such that the service He provides would first be FOR me, then flow THROUGH me. When we fail to first receive from God's unlimited source of love, we end up giving from our own limited supply and become depleted. This dysfunctional state of existence was never God's intention for us as His divine daughters. Scripture declares, "For we know how dearly God loves us, because He has given us the Holy Spirit to fill our hearts with His love." (Romans 5:5 NLT)

God first fills our hearts with the eternal wellspring of His love that never runs dry. Then we are empowered by the Holy Spirit, who gives us this eternal love, to love others. 1 John 4:19 (NLT) declares, "We love each other because God loved us FIRST."

What does the love He has for me look like?

- *RIGHTEOUSNESS that secures my eternal relationship with God as His beloved daughter*
- *FORGIVENESS and MERCY that covers my sins and faults, and redeems my guilt and shame*
- *GRACE and PATIENCE that covers my inadequacies as I wrestle with my imperfections*
- *COMPASSION and COMFORT that embraces my brokenness and heals my hurts*
- *HONOR and GLORY that considers me precious, grants me strength, and guarantees my victory (1 Peter 5:4)*

Prayer:

ABBA, as I remember that you are FOR ME, and then flow THROUGH ME, empower me to...

- *Use your righteousness to share your love*
- *Use your mercy to give others forgiveness*
- *Use your patience to grant others grace*
- *Use your compassion to provide others with comfort*
- *Use your glory to honor others*

ABBA, be FOR ME, then flow THROUGH ME.
In Jesus name. Amen.

"Now may the God of peace—who brought up from the dead, our Lord Jesus, the great Shepherd of the sheep, and ratified an eternal covenant with his blood—may he equip you with all you need for doing his will. May He produce in you, through the power of Jesus Christ, every good thing that is pleasing to Him. All glory to Him forever and ever! Amen." Hebrews 13:20-21 NLT

Love and blessings
–Rev. Dr. Teleah Phillips

Name ways you have depleted yourself by not filling yourself up first with love and personal care.

Name ways you can start working on yourself by taking care of your personal needs first, so you will be able to better share these gifts with others.

Week 26

"From everyone who has been given much, much will be demanded; and from the one who has been entrusted with much, much more will be asked."

Luke 12:48 NIV

I love that scripture. I think of it often. Probably because I feel it applies to me. Not to me alone, but to me personally. I feel as though that verse is speaking directly to me. Do you ever feel that way about something you hear or something you read? That verse just grabs me for some reason.

I'm not sure why I feel that way, because I'm certainly not rich. I don't have a large house or a boat or an airplane, but it seems I have everything I need. I look around and I wonder why I'm so blessed. Yes. Blessed. That's it! I know there are others who have way more material things than I do, but I think it's not all about that. Maybe it's about what you have in your heart. Maybe we're supposed to think and look beyond what's right in front of our faces.

Maybe you haven't even realized you're so blessed. Yet. Maybe right now you're starting to think about it. What if, instead of material things to give away, you gave away kindness... or encouragement... or inspiration? That's a great idea! How many people can you influence today with your kindness or encouragement or inspiration? After all, what we've all been given is the power to influence someone else in a positive way. That's the real gift. And you've got it. Yes, you! You've got the power; you've got the means to help someone else. And by you giving it away to someone else, it just means that it is replenished in your heart by a thousand-fold. There's no end!

Maybe that's why I like that verse so much. I've got so much to give, gifts that were given to me, and they never run out! It's amazing. And we all have it. It's inside each and every one of us. That's what I believe. That's what that verse means to me. You've got it in you to do great things. Maybe not with material possessions, but with what's in your heart. That's a beautiful thought. And you're a beautiful person. I believe it, with all my heart. I believe in God, and God believes in you and me. I love that thought. I hope you do, too.

–Sharon Esworthy Wheeler

Name 5 gifts you were given that you can pass onto to the world.

1.
2.
3.
4.
5.

When you have given away these gifts, how did it make you feel?

Week 27

"And those who were seen dancing were thought to be insane by those who could not hear the music."

–Attributed to Friedrich Nietzsche. 2005 February 8, The Ledger, Section: East Polk, They Said It, Page F4, Lakeland, Florida. (NewsBank Access World News)

Have you ever had a moment in time when you knew instantly that your life would be changed forever? That experience happened to me New Year's Eve 2004, when I woke up to find a lump under my arm, and at that moment, I knew my life would never be the same. I had three children under the age of four, the youngest being three months old, and my husband was working sixty-plus hours a week so I could be a stay-at-home mom. Thus, this health crisis put a strain on our situation but we made it! We made it through two bouts of breast cancer in four years, and we are stronger because of it.

I became an avid learner of health, wellness and prevention as a result of this health crisis, and I began to help others with the necessary tools to stay healthy. I became obsessed with personal development. Humans have a great ability to change, but sometimes we do not realize we need the change until we get a nudge from life. And hopefully we recognize that nudge!!

But most of all, this crisis in my life led me to be present and have compassion for others. We never really know what people are going through in their lives. Did the guy who just cut me off on the road do it because he was racing to get his pregnant wife to the hospital? Did the lady who was rude to me just learn that her father died this morning? Did the person who forgot about our appointment and is not responding to my texts just find out they have a terminal disease, or their kid got in trouble at school? We just do not know, and so compassion and grace are key. Knowing that what people do is about them and not about us is so important, and always giving them the benefit of the doubt. Most people are not trying to hurt us; they are just trying to live this thing we call life.

What have you changed in your life due to a crisis?

Think of times when you realized compassion was the answer to a situation.

Write a note to those people, letting them know you care (if possible).

Be Love, Be Well & Be Fabulous,
–*Susie*

Name 5 moments when you knew your life would change forever.

1.
2.
3.
4.
5.

How did those circumstances change you, and what knowledge did you gain from them?

WEEK 28

Talitha Koum

Standing in front of my high school speech class, tears started to build up in my eyes. I was paralyzed with fear. Unable to see the notecards in my hand or stop shaking, I made the decision to just sit down in utter embarrassment, and there I sat silently. I had no voice. Fear of what other people would think, fear of failure, fear of my inadequacies ruled over my life. I continued to drift along in quiet compliance for most of my adulthood until I had an encounter with God, who grabbed me by the hand and said, "Love these women. Tell them of my passion for them. I'm sending you." A simple but daily yes started me on a journey I was completely unqualified for: co-founding a nonprofit, and developing programming to reach and offer rescue to women trapped in human trafficking.

He took this girl who was terrified to drive down inner-city streets and transformed her into one who searches alleys to hand a woman a rose to remind her she is beautiful and has a purpose. From submissive to outspoken, I get to speak to lawmakers and law enforcers, elevating the voices of women and defending them against unfair laws. I share at churches and events about this mission of God and invite them into it. There is no part of me that is capable of any of this. Rather, He is the one that brings the dead to life, real life. Whether you are dead in addiction and prostitution or dead in fear and silence, just grab His hand.

In partnership with God, I get to tell the story of this tattoo on my arm, "Talitha Koum," to a beloved princess at the drop-in center:

"When they came from the house of Jairus and said, 'Your daughter is dead. Why bother the teacher [Jesus] anymore?' He replied, 'Don't be afraid; just believe.'... Taking her by the hand, Jesus said, 'Talitha koum!' which means, 'Little girl, I say to you arise.'" (Mark 5:14 ESV)

And with a big smile on my face, I say, "That's going to be my story!"

–*Tiffany Tripp*

Name 5 times in your life when you were paralyzed by fear.

1.
2.
3.
4.
5.

Say what happened when you put your trust in your higher power.

Week 29

There is always something to be grateful for.

I grew up with an emotionally and physically abusive father. As much as my mom tried to shield me and my brother from the harsh words and abuse, it left a lasting impression and mental impact on me. For years, my mode of thinking was always, "I'm not good enough or smart enough... I have so many flaws... Why would anyone love me? Why would anyone actually listen to what I say or think?" My mom (who is my hero), and my husband (my rock), did everything in their power to sway my thoughts and beliefs in myself, but I just couldn't move past my feelings of inadequacy and fear. Through therapy and a renewed relationship with God, I began to view things differently. The things I have learned over the last several years have completely changed my outlook and opinion of myself.

First and foremost, I look to the Lord. I can't tell you how many times I have dropped to my knees and prayed when I didn't know what to do or how to react. We must admit we are not perfect, yet God still loves us. He sent His son to die for us; therefore, we are worthy of grace and forgiveness! Learn to appreciate the good in others and tell them, daily, the impact they have on you. A kind word may not make a big difference to you, but it can mean the world to them. Each day wake up and name three things you are grateful for. Some days will be harder than others, but always find three things to thank the Lord for. Lastly, learn to ask for help, and never be ashamed of needing guidance.

I lost my dad two months ago, and I had a lot of shame, grief and guilt to work through. When we don't deal with feelings, they come back and cause an almost suffocating grief. I knew I needed my counselor, along with time and prayers from family and friends to move on. Forgive yourself for your flaws and, in doing so, forgive those who have harmed or hurt you, just as God forgave us. You will not believe the peace and freedom forgiveness grants you! You ARE worth loving and you ARE worthy! Surround yourself with likeminded and positive people and watch the impact it will have on your life!

"For I know the thoughts I have toward you, saith the Lord, thoughts of peace, and not of evil, to give you and expected end." Jeremiah 29:11 (KJV)

–*Chicky Dyer*

Name old thought patterns you have held about yourself that are not true. How have they made you feel?

____

____

____

____

____

Name ways you can choose to view these circumstances differently and work on healing yourself.

____

____

____

____

____

____

Week 30

You have a Great Purpose

"For we walk by faith, not by sight" - II Cor. 5:7

It was summer of 1993; I was seventeen years old and excited to be heading off to college. I was ready for new adventures and to not be in a small town anymore. At the snap of a finger, my life changed forever, and nothing would ever be the same.

I let who I thought was "the love of my life," who looked like Leonardo De Caprio at that time, drive the car my parents blessed me with. The night ended in a tragic way, leaving me in pain for many years and causing my parents much stress.

That night, I was the passenger in my car as it flipped four times, breaking every bone in my face and jaw, and entangling my braces. My friends were scared, not knowing whether to pull me out of the car or leave me. I know I should have died that night! There were many hard, sad and unbelievable days that summer, and for the next few years as I had multiple surgeries. I had so many sleepless nights, along with physically, mentally and emotionally exhausting days, just doing what used to be daily normal activities. But God had a great purpose for me, and He does for you too.

God works in great ways. About nine months before this tragic accident, my orthodontist sent me to a maxillofacial surgeon, Dr. C, to get a consult. It was after his office had closed for the day that Dr. C said, "Sure let's get the molds and x-rays for the consult." Later that week, I told my mom I did not want the procedures the orthodontist recommended, so she let it be.

While in the hospital, a plastic surgeon came to see me, and I was so upset by what he was recommending. I wanted to look like me, not someone else. My mom contacted Dr. C to ask if he could come visit me. He had all the dental molds and panoramic x-rays from months before to put my facial bones back together. Thank you, Jesus! Dr. C and Dr. G did my maxillofacial surgeries that resulted in me having twelve titanium plates and fifteen screws, which are still in my face today.

Despite the tragedies, I was bound and determined to pursue college and did not want to get trapped in a small town, where lots of people were only focused on things that are negative and bring people down. I knew God had a great purpose for me.

I went to college, joined a sorority, made new, wonderful friends and earned by BSN in nursing and a minor in business management. I kept trying to have a relationship with my old flame, but God had a different plan even though I could not see it.

It was about twenty-three years later in April of 2016 that my brother told me, "Oh, by the way, your old flame is into drugs, in and out of jail, and barely has a tooth left in his mouth." It was all I needed to hear. Thank you Jesus for protecting me from what I thought I wanted and blessing me with so much that I did not know I needed!

We have II COR 5:7 etched in every part of our boutique business now. "For we walk by faith, not by sight." I remind myself of this daily and what it truly means. I am trusting every detail of my life to The Lord and know that He has my best interest at heart. Yes, many days are hard and challenging, and things do not always go as I have planned. It is the unexpected things, the part of life that happens in a split second, that changes our course forever. That season of life was hard and challenging during the summer of 1993, and I knew I should have died that night. By the grace of God, He had the pieces in place for Dr. C to have what he needed for me medically. God knew my life was not meant to go down the road of drugs and alcohol in a relationship with the wrong person. He had a much greater purpose for me. So, although the crisis that summer was traumatic, after twenty-three years I understood it.

On Memorial Day weekend 2020, it was amazing to cross paths with both of Dr. C and Dr. G, who performed my multiple maxillofacial surgeries. Both showed up in our boutique in Florida, and it was beyond emotional, as you can imagine! I am forever grateful to these amazing surgeons!

When things are challenging, remember, God brings people into your life for a reason and takes them out for a reason, even if we don't understand why. This tragic lesson taught me to never take life for granted and that each day is a gift. It brought me out of a small town and pushed me to do greater things for the Glory of God. May this inspire you, that if you come through a tragic life event, to trust God's control and walk by faith, not by sight.

–Kristi R

Name past traumatic events in your life that you thought you might never recover from.

____

____

____

Now that time has passed and you can look back on these events, are you able to see possible blessings they may have brought you?

____

____

____

____

WEEK 31

"Being a mother is learning about strengths you didn't know you had and dealing with fears you didn't know existed."

—Wooten, Linda. "Mothers Thoughts." First edition, Winston-Derek Pub, 1990.

I am thankful I come from a strong mother. As little girls, we love and worship our fathers. Teenage years happen. While we are growing into women, we usually think our moms don't know anything. As we grow and experience life, we begin to realize just how much our mothers have done. We begin to see the amazing strength our moms have every day for our families. We start looking at ourselves to see if we have acquired the qualities our moms have shown us.

My mom grew bigger than life in my eyes. Then a mother's biggest fear happened, and my little brother died at the age of eighteen. I watched a strong lady fall to her knees. I watched and wondered how she would ever get through it. But she was still a mother. She dealt with her fear. She had two other children who needed her strength. So, she found it within herself. She was strong but hurting, and she didn't think she'd ever smile again. When her first grandchild was born, her world brightened. For me, the daughter of this strong woman, I found myself wondering if I had her strength. Could I be the mother she was to me? The wisdom I gained from my mother was a gift. I raised my son with confidence. As time passed, the unthinkable happened. My mother lost another son, my brother. She was grief-stricken, I was heartbroken and my twelve-year-old son was absolutely devastated. My mom again showed us what it is to be a mother. She picked herself up once again. Now as a mother, I show my son the strength my mother showed me. She taught me well. I am still fearful as moms will be, but I know how to face those fears. I know how to look inside and find a mother's strength.

I am grateful to have been raised by a strong mother. As little girls it's natural to love and worship our fathers. Then, teenage years happen. As we grow into women, seeking our own independence and believing our moms do not know anything, we do not consider at one time they too were our age.

–*Anonymous*

Name 5 strengths you have learned from your mother and how they molded you.

1.
2.
3.
4.
5.

Name 5 ways you can pass on these strengths to others.

1.
2.
3.
4.
5.

Week 32

To truly LOVE someone is to SERVE

Throughout my life I had some great examples of how to serve others. My dad was a single father to me and my older siblings. I watched and learned how he gave of himself daily: to his job; to his work at home, cleaning, laundry; and ensuring we had everything we needed. As I grew up, and my Dad became ill with lung cancer, I took care of him for the first time. I learned during that time how to never lose hope, how to keep pushing forward, and how to not take anything for granted.

Two years later, I enrolled into the nursing program. I learned a new skill set and how to serve others with medicine, critical thinking and proper handwashing. I learned how to save lives and how serving is sometimes just simply holding a hand.

Nearly five years after nursing school began, I got married and started a family. Our first baby, Joseph, was diagnosed with Trisomy 13, a rare chromosomal disorder that causes heart, brain and lung defects. He lived only six precious days, during which I had very little sleep, afraid to miss a second of his little life. I learned how to serve while my heart was breaking.

Now, I have worked nine years as a nurse, with three little girls—six, four, and two—and a husband and a home. With laundry piling up and a sink full of dishes, serving has been taken to a whole new level! After taking care of people all day, the only "me" time is for fifteen minutes in the shower or at night when I close my eyes. Taking care of others all day, every day, with no time to yourself can be extremely difficult. One day as I contemplated getting in my car, driving away and never looking back, I closed my eyes, with tears streaming down my face, and said, "God, I can't do this anymore. Life's too hard!" I heard Him ask me a question: "What does it mean to TRULY love someone?" And I responded, "I don't know, the Bible says that there's no greater love than laying down your life for your friends (John15:13). And Jesus died on the cross and gave His life for us. So, I guess to truly love someone is to die for them?" And the Lord answered, "To TRULY love someone, is to SERVE." My entire perspective changed in that moment. I'm not just folding laundry, picking up toys and cooking dinner. I'm loving my family! I'm not just taking care of the sick and the elderly... I'm showing them a kind of love like no other.

Maybe your first thought of being fierce isn't serving by being a stay-at-home mom or wiping butts and taking care of the dying. But on the contrary, there is NOTHING more fierce than giving your whole heart and soul, your time and life, to serving others. We may not have time for ourselves, right now, but those days will come. One life at a time, one day at a time, we are changing the world for the better. We're not just moms, we're superheroes! We're not just nurses, we're the heart and soul of health care. So, tighten your mom bun and LOVE your family like no one else can. No one else can love them the way you do. Service with a smile takes on a whole new meaning now, doesn't it.

–Tracy

Name 5 ways you felt you were killing yourself for others, but you now see that you are really loving them by serving them.

1.
2.

3.
4.
5.

Name 5 ways you were served. How did it make you feel loved?

1.
2.
3.
4.
5.

Week 33

Crafted to Serve

I remember the first time I went through a class on spiritual gifts, I left feeling more lost than when I started. Perhaps I was still too young in my faith, or still too young in years. Either way, it was years later when my brother-in-law, a pastor, mentioned in passing how God had blessed me with the gift of hospitality. At first, I thought he was joking! I mean, I knew I enjoyed entertaining guests and organizing family and social gatherings, but I certainly never thought of it as a "gift." I think I had just always been in awe of those who had the gift of prophecy, teaching or leadership—you know, the obvious ones! But after that day, I truly felt like I found my "place." I took that gift to heart and have tried to utilize it to the best of my ability ever since.

Fast forward a handful of years... My husband and I started a hobby, making wine in our basement. We'd share the wine with friends, take it to parties, and give it as gifts during the holidays. After receiving overwhelming support and encouragement, we decided to open our own small winery and tasting room.

Little did we know how that gift of hospitality would help take a tiny little side business into what it is today. We chose the motto "Crafted to Serve," because not only are all our products hand-crafted and meant to be served and shared with others, but we also believe that as children of God, we have been skillfully crafted to serve one another.

Have you found your "place"? Maybe it's your purpose, or maybe it's your gift. We all have something that God uniquely crafted us for. Find what that is for you!

–Tonya M

Name 5 gifts you have that you could share with the world.

1.
2.
3.
4.
5.

Name 5 gifts others have told you that you have and could share with the world.

1.
2.
3.
4.
5.

WEEK 34

I am not sure what God has planned for me today, but I will trust in His leadership and follow in His direction.

I have been blessed with so much love, health and success in my life, and often I feel unworthy. It is in these times that I recognize the devil is at work, and I know I need to regroup, concentrating on what I know is real. I have learned that forgiveness and hope are things you can only get from one source: your Holy Father.

I am a product of an Appalachian town. Divorced parents, free lunches, pregnant before graduating high school. Married and divorced within two years and only in my twenties; I was living as a single mother with a son.

Looking through my son's eyes, he truly loved me, and I adored him. But all I could see were my failures. I grew up watching The Brady Bunch and Little House on the Prairie, and everything always turned out for them. I was almost deceived into believing these television shows were actual reality.

We beat ourselves up for all the mistakes we make in life and find it hard to forgive ourselves, when in all fairness, those mistakes, are what makes us who we are.

Fast forward twenty years. I now have five beautiful, healthy boys. They are growing up in an instant. Seeing them, I know I did something right. I truly hope looking back, that I will have lived up to all their expectations of a mother.

I have always tried hard to live the best life for me and my family, and always putting them ahead of myself.

We, as women, lose sight of ourselves and our dreams as we build and mold our children for success. I pride myself on helping and smiling at others. Fighting to continue to have a positive outlook on every situation.

I would like for YOU to focus forward on your life and stop looking back. It doesn't matter where you were born... You can achieve whatever you set your sights on. What I thought at the time were unforgivable mistakes were just my steppingstones, and those can catapult people to a new level when they just have faith.

–Stacy Bowman

Name 5 mistakes you made when you were young that you constantly beat yourself up about.

1.
2.
3.
4.
5.

Share the ways these mistakes were steppingstones to make you who you are today.

____

____

____

____

____

____

____

Week 35

If you are not happy, make a change. You ALWAYS have a choice, and life is too short to not choose happiness.

One thing I have learned in life is that women really are the same, no matter where we are from. We all face challenges in life, we all have struggles and we all have choices. It is how we react to those challenges and struggles that make us the unique people we are. No doubt, my past has thrown enough obstacles at me to take down even the strongest of women, except maybe Mother Teresa! Through all those times, I have always had a choice about how I would ultimately respond to those difficulties, and today, those same choices guide everything I do.

I choose to be strong. I choose to be empowered. I choose to be at the center of change. I choose to be a leader. I choose to set a positive example. I choose to be happy. I choose to surround myself with people I love, and who love me back. And if I had to choose one quote I live by, there wouldn't be just one. The following would all be on my list:

- *Life really is what you make it, and if you live by the belief that your glass is always half empty... you will never be able to fill your cup.*
- *Surround yourself with the types of people you want to emulate.*
- *Be passionate about everything you do, and relentlessly pursue your dreams.*
- *Never let fear stand in your way of accomplishing success. If you*

cower down and refuse to go after whatever it is that you want... you will never know if you could have achieved that seemingly unattainable goal, because you never tried. If you don't ask, you won't get, and the answer will always be no. But if you have the courage to ask, the answer could actually be yes. So, go after everything you want, and be fearless!

–*Krista L. Guagenti*

Name 5 choices you would like to make that could improve your life, but you have put off because you're paralyzed by fear.

1.
2.
3.
4.
5.

Name 5 possible events that could happen to you if you choose to stay stuck in fear and not make the choice for change.

1.
2.
3.
4.
5.

Name 5 possible events that could happen to you if you choose to move forward in faith and make a choice to face your fear.

1.

2.
3.
4.
5.

WEEK 36

Don't be afraid of change. Change makes us grow. The only way to change is if we learn and are exposed to new and exciting things.

I am a girl who is always on the go. Being happy and content has always been important to me. Life is good, and I say whatever you want, don't wait around... go for it!

I've traveled and lived in different areas, where I've met so many amazing people. I started out really wanting to do some traveling before I settled down and maybe one day have kids. So, one day I decided to just go for it! I would pack my bags and just do it! I knew if I didn't take this chance, I would always have the "what-ifs." At that time, I was between jobs and decided I would leave Ohio and make Arizona my new home. This was it! I was going to take the leap!

I had a dear work friend move to Arizona a few years prior, which was an incentive to go. Not to mention, it was sunny more than three hundred days a year, and I love hot weather! Plus, it was far away from everything I knew... It was just the chance I needed to take!

Later, my travels would take me from Arizona to Alabama. The lifestyle change from being out west with mountains was a huge change but the beach was beautiful too! I ended up living in Alabama for over a year, and then moved back to Ohio due to an immediate family member's illness.

Shortly after I moved back to Ohio, I ended up getting married and having a child. The decision to travel was one of the best that I have ever made! I met a ton of amazing people and I was fortunate to experience life in totally different areas. Traveling definitely made me more well-rounded as a person and I would absolutely do it all over again! The only thing I would add is to spend a year in NYC.

Everyone has a different story, and each one is so unique! I say, 'believe in yourself and be your own inspiration!' You can do whatever you want! Now is your time...

–Tracy Delancey Culver

Name 5 changes that you have been wanting to make in your life, but you have let fear stop you.

1.
2.
3.
4.
5.

Name 5 positive outcomes that could happen if you dared to move forward and make the changes, despite the fear.

1.
2.
3.
4.
5.

WEEK 37

Everyone has a story to tell. I believe in staying strong when things fall apart. When life knocks you down, you must dig deep, find your strength and get back up.

Like many, I have been shaken to my core with life's challenges. I lost my dad to cancer, watched helplessly as my mom went through a series of mental breakdowns, went through a divorce, lost a thirty-year established career due to bankruptcy and most recently lost my stepson to suicide.

I've experienced many stages of grief and uncertainty and had my faith challenged. Yet my faith, determination, hope and stubbornness have all gotten me through my darkest days. It's cliché I know, but you really don't know how strong you are until 'strong' is all that you have to hold onto.

Many mornings I have looked into my mirror and asked myself, "Where do I go from here?" In those moments, I say to my reflection, "If He leads you to it, He will see you through it." I believe it, I cherish it and I live it.

Just remember, your pain, your mistakes and your past do not define who you are. They're steppingstones to guide you towards the next evolution of you.

You can always rewrite your story and be the person you are meant to be. Life is short, our days are precious and nothing is prettier than a beautiful smile and a kind heart. Think big, believe in yourself and never give up. Life can and will be a challenge—focus on what you can control, and find the blessings in everyday life.

Live your best life.

–Paula

Name events in your life that have knocked you down.

Name 5 strengths you have developed through your faith in a higher power that have pulled you through these events.

1.
2.
3.
4.
5.

Week 38

Grace in the Wilderness

"Thus says the LORD: 'The people who survived the sword found grace in the wilderness—Israel, when I went to give him rest.'"

Jeremiah 31:2

This scripture refers to the grace God showed Israel in their wanderings in the wilderness after He so miraculously brought them out of Egypt and set them on their journey to the Promised Land.

Throughout the journey—which should have taken days, but ended up taking decades due to their complaining and rebellious ways—God continuously provided for their every need. He fed them manna from heaven and water from the rock, their shoes never wore out and they were protected from the sun and the heat.

God could have destroyed them all for their disobedience and sin, and, indeed, as a result an entire generation never saw the Promised Land. However, God showed them grace. He did so because of the covenant with Abraham, and His everlasting love.

"The LORD has appeared of old to me, saying: 'Yes, I have loved you with an everlasting love; therefore, with lovingkindness I have drawn you." Jeremiah 31:3.

Eventually a new generation went into the Promised Land. Have you ever found yourself wandering about 'in the wilderness' of life? Have you ever felt as though you were in a period of drought in your spiritual life? Perhaps you know the reason: You've not been drinking from the waters of His Spirit or feeding your soul from His Word, the Bread of Life. However, other times you may be having a wilderness experience simply because of the hard knocks of life: loss of a job or financial hardship; health, family, or relationship issues; stress or exhaustion; spiritual, emotional, or mental battles of mind or heart.

God knows where you're at and what you are going through. He loves you with an everlasting love. He desires to give you grace in the wilderness.

Will you ask for His grace to be poured on you today? If you do, you'll find He'll lead you to green and pleasant pastures, a place of promise, provision and peace.

–Kim Batson

Name 5 times you have found yourself wondering in the wilderness of life feeling lost.

1.
2.
3.
4.
5.

Name 5 ways you can turn over your hardships to God and let Him guide you to your destination.

1.
2.
3.
4.
5.

Week 39

"Rejoice with me, I have found my lost sheep."

Luke 15:6 NIV

For many years I felt like the lone, lost sheep in Luke 15:3. I didn't feel like anyone was looking for me when I was being trafficked, and that God didn't care about me. I moved around a lot as a kid, and although I came from a large, Catholic family, I didn't have a support network and just followed the norm that had been set in each new place in order to get along. I always had a strong urging that God had a special calling for me, but I had no idea what it was. I also held the secret of what was happening to me, being sold to others, and I vowed never to tell a soul.

Years later, after I had escaped and became a social worker, I started to heal, and an amazing thing happened to me. I was driving to work one morning from the country into the city, and I turned the corner of a huge barren field. I saw a large, white, fluffy sheep walking in a perfectly straight line, and at least ten smaller sheep followed it. The line was so perfect, and a sense of peace swept over me. I was astounded that they could walk that straight, and I thought, "Where are they going? Why are they just following that one?' It perplexed me all the way to my office.

I didn't see it at the time, but it was a sign that I would soon be called to be that leader: a shepherd. It was later that year that I started my ministry of helping find children who are being trafficked like I had been, and I began to help survivors heal. Now I ask other survivors (God's sheep) to allow me to lead them, to follow me to a beautiful place where we can accept His unconditional love for us. For many years I felt like I wasn't worthy to be found or rejoiced. Now I am humbled that He chose this calling for me, because even just ONE "sheep" matters and should be rejoiced when found.

–Theresa Flores

Have you ever felt so lost you had given up hope?

____

____

____

____

____

What signs are around you that show you God is speaking to you?

____

____

____

____

____

____

Not everyone needs to be a leader; we need followers too. What is your role?

____

____

____

____

____

____

Week 40

Miracles Happen Every Day

"No one is useless in this world who lightens the burdens of another."

–Dickens, Charles. "Doctor Marigold." United States, Dodo Press, 2007.

"You have breast cancer."

Words no woman wants to hear. Especially twice. After ten years of being cancer free, it had returned.

Since I had faced this before, it seemed easier the second time to determine a battle (treatment) plan with my ever-supportive husband. But that's where the similarity ended. Surgery was more extensive, and chemotherapy and radiation treatments were more exhausting. Many days it was hard to muster any energy. And that's when a miracle (or two or three) would happen. A meal, a special dessert, a homemade card, a text, a phone call or a visitor would appear. My husband, daughters, friends, family and strangers energized me with each act of kindness, large or small. These miracle workers carried me when I could not carry myself. Every day they inspire me to be that miracle worker!

–Cathy Korikian

Reflect over your life and name small miracles that have happened to you.

Name ways you can brighten another's day by acts of kindness.

Week 41

Have appreciation rather than expectations. Life has a way of taking you where you're supposed to go. Just trust in God and have patience!

In my life I've been exposed to things I never should have been, including physical, verbal, and emotional abuse. After time, I started to believe there was something wrong with me. I felt I was nothing and began to treat myself like I didn't matter. I began drinking heavily and became very promiscuous. I didn't love myself and used to think nobody else would either. Looking back now, I realize how fortunate I am that I wasn't a victim of human trafficking. As a single mom of two beautiful children, I made mistakes—big ones. I wasn't always the best mom and would sometimes take out my frustrations on my children—not in a physical way, but they definitely felt the brunt of my feelings of inadequacy. I loved them so very much, but I would sometimes blame the fact that I had them, for my life not turning out the way I wanted it to. It took me a very long time to figure out that it's ok to make mistakes. We don't have to be perfect. Nobody is. We're all human, after all. We do the best we can.

The important thing is to learn from our mistakes and grow in a positive direction. I've learned that rather than having expectations, we should have appreciation. Once we begin to see all we have and come to truly appreciate it, the fog is lifted and the lens through which we look at life is finally clear. My children (and grandchildren) have turned out amazing, despite all my mistakes. We have a great relationship and enjoy spending time together regularly. Once I started gaining confidence and becoming comfortable in my own skin, I met my wonderful husband.

You know that Rascal Flatts song, "God Bless the Broken Road?" Well, I believe God had a plan for me all along and led me along the broken road right to where I am supposed to be. He has a way of doing that. I'm not sure what I ever did to deserve him, but I am so thankful for whatever it was.

–Jacque Annarino

Name 5 times you expected a situation to turn out a certain way and you tried to control the outcome. How did that turn out?

1.
2.
3.
4.
5.

Name 5 situations you turned over to your higher power and describe the outcome and how you felt.

1.
2.
3.
4.
5.

Week 42

"To Hear the Call
Listen, Listen, all and all
Quiet that sound from them all
Hear the echoes chanting calls forever embedded within the skull
Listen, Listen to the call
Hear the Whisper to it all"

–Author, Gloria Y. Endicott 5/14/2017

To all the courageous women out there: Know, you are never alone, as within, your light guides and protects you. The light of love. Sometimes we forget about the light that dwells within us, and we become fearful due to our past. Recognizing the difference allows you to move from your past to your future. Trusting and listening to your inner voice will allow the light of love to guide you and move you towards your future. For my personal journey, I quiet the noise from them all by regressing through meditation practices, nature, and affirmations of self-love. I reflect when the past creeps up without criticizing it; instead I recognize my emotions, feelings and fears and then release them back to the past and return to my future in the present moment of now.

–Gloria Y. Endicott

Name 5 fears of your past that may be controlling your future.

1.
2.
3.
4.
5.

Name ways you can listen to your inner voice and allow your light and love to guide you into the future.

Week 43

"I have not been given a spirit of fear."

2 Timothy 1:7(KJV)

I don't consider myself a fear-laden person, but I am familiar with this unwanted presence. As a small-business owner, I've had a multitude of opportunities for fear to rear its ugly head. I've experienced fear of failure, fear of not measuring up, fear of all the unknown, fear of nobody showing up, fear of an impending difficult conversation. There are situations I often feel unprepared for, that I'm not sure I'm equipped to handle, that beckon me to play small. After feeling these emotions, hope begins to rise, as I proclaim, like in 2 Timothy 1:7, "God has not given me a spirit of fear, but of power, love, and sound judgment." I can channel peace when I remember that I am not bound by the way I feel, as I take hold of the power I'm entitled to as a daughter of God.

On a deeper level, I've recently experienced a traumatic loss—one that has forever changed me, my family dynamic and what I envision aspects of my future will look like. It is so easy to give way to fear, to let circumstances draw us to it. Most of the time I experience this fear as I think about the future. I take my thoughts captive and remind myself I do not have to worry about tomorrow; I have the strength I need for today. I receive this strength as I commit daily to abide in the source of my strength. This is a daily practice. So, yes, fear is real and often shows up, but it's not who I am and not the spirit I claim.

If you experience fear, I encourage you to speak this mantra to yourself and allow peace to wash over you and hope to rise up within you.

–Laura

Name 5 fears that sometimes paralyze you from moving forward in life.

1.
2.
3.
4.
5.

Name ways you can connect with your higher power and put your trust in that guidance so you can live for today.

Week 44

"You are here to decide if your life, relationships and world are true and beautiful enough for you. And if they are not and you dare to admit they are not, you must decide if you have the guts, the right–perhaps even the duty–to burn to the ground that which is not true and beautiful enough and get started building what is."

–Doyle, Glennon. "Untamed". United States: The Dial Press, 2020.

I have many strong, wonderful adjectives to describe myself, but spontaneous or even risky do not appear anywhere on that list. During the first few days of May 2018, I planned to move to St. Louis to be with my boyfriend of two years. I was prepared to find a teaching job in the public school system. However, on May 10th the relationship ended. Instead of moving to St. Louis, I moved to Austin, Texas, after speaking with the principal who interviewed me and in less than sixty minutes convinced me to teach 6th grade ELA at her school. I didn't know a single person in Austin, but I have to say this was the most exhilarating twenty-four hours of my life!

Prior to this, life in Charlotte, North Carolina, had not been easy for me. I was seeking a life filled with joy, success and meaning, but it did not work out that way for me. I found myself teaching in a toxic environment that produced an ongoing lack of concern for the children, and many did not value what I brought to the table as a teacher. I had a desire to be a confident woman who prided herself on being a fierce woman, displaying a boldness to go after what I wanted. So, I moved away.

I'm grateful my life in Austin, Texas is refreshing and beautiful. I have been recognized as Teacher of the Year at a school that is truly creating life-changing opportunities for underserved students. I have a group of friends who support me tirelessly. I am in love with a man who challenges me to be the strongest and best version of myself every day. I owe everything to the courage that nudged me to move here, because we, as women, have the duty to create and protect beautiful and true worlds for ourselves.

–Hannah Orth

Name different parts of your life you may not be living to the fullest, due to fear or other life circumstances. How does that make you feel?

____

____

____

____

____

____

____

Now begin to dream and imagine conquering your fears and daring to take a chance to move forward. How does that make you feel?

____

____

____

____

____

____

____

____

Week 45

I'm good with me!

I remember as a little girl always wanting to be the best at everything I did. I thought that was the key to happiness in life. I thought my family, friends and even my boss would like or RESPECT me more if I were the best.

I remember being so upset at myself because I could not figure out my homework. My mom sat me down on the couch and put her hands on my knees and looked me in the eyes and said, "You can be or do anything you put your mind to." Who knew that would be the game changer for me? That day will forever be a defining moment in my life.

I wish I could say I held those words close to my heart always, and I didn't let life get me down, but that's not always the case. Life is full of highs and lows, but it's how you handle those situations that really defines who you are.

One of my best friends once told me that I did not always have to be the strong one for my friends and family, but I could rely on them as well for support. I could let my guard down and trust that true friends would not judge me. My boss once told me I was letting my W-2 define me and that I was worth way more than what was on that piece of paper. My parents would constantly say I needed to slow down and enjoy life before it passed me by. It's not about what everyone else thinks but about what I know.

I've come a long way from that little girl on the couch. I believe we are all here for a reason... and my purpose is not to be the best in everyone else's eyes, but to be the best that I can be for MYSELF.

I'm good with me!

–Kimberly Regan

Name ways in which you thought you had to be perfect in order to gain yours and other peoples' respect.

How do you feel when you have learned to love and accept yourself, imperfections and all?

Week 46

Overcoming Grief and Sorrow

While we struggle through uncertain times, one constant is God's love and guidance for navigating hardships. I am reminded of a writing in the Baha'i faith.

> *"Grief and sorrow do not come to us by chance, they are sent to us by the Divine Mercy for our own perfecting"*
>
> *–Abdu'l-Bahá, Paris Talks/Part One: 14 The Benefits of God to Man, p. 51-52.*

My life has included great joy, but trials too. At seventeen, I left home, lost my chance for a higher education and was on my own. I married young and, at times worked two jobs, all the while trying to have children for ten years and could not. I helped put my husband through college, and then he left me for my best friend. Through all of this, several family members with whom I was very close passed away.

My situation is not unique. We all experience joy and hardships in our lives. Another writing that has molded my faith and shaped my life is the following:

> *"He urges you to persevere and add up your accomplishments, rather than to dwell on the dark side of things... turn your back to the darkness and your face to Me."*
>
> –Shoghi Effendi, From a letter Written on behalf of Shoghi Effendi, 22 October 1949, in Unfolding Destiny, p. 457.

But my faith has always given me the perspective that tests, like these in life, provide a benefit.

> *"We must always look ahead and seek to accomplish in the future what we may have failed to do in the past. Failures, tests, and trials, if we use them correctly, can become the means of purifying our spirit, strengthening our characters and enable us to rise to greater heights of service."*
>
> –From a letter Written on behalf of Shoghi Effendi, 14 December 1941, In Lights of Guidance, p. 601, no 2039.

So, I look back at all my hardships and have learned that walking a path of service to humanity is the key. This passage tells us how.

> *"Be not the slave of your moods, but their master. But if you are so angry, so depressed and so sore that your spirit cannot find deliverance and peace even in prayer, then quickly go and give some pleasure to someone lowly or sorrowful, or to a guilty or innocent sufferer! Sacrifice yourself, your talent, your time, your rest to another, to one who has to bear a heavier load than you – and your unhappy mood will dissolve into a blessed, contented submission to God."*
>
> –Attributed to 'Abdu'l-Baha - The Research Department has found that these words were attributed to Abdu'l-Baha in an unpublished English translation of notes in German by Dr. Josephine Fallscheer taken on 5 August 1910. As the statement is a pilgrim note, it cannot be authenticated.

My mantra is: "Be generous in prosperity, and thankful in adversity." Be kind to all people and love them with a pure spirit; be humble, make someone laugh, smile at a stranger, bring food to the hungry, and pray for inspiration.

> —Inspired from a Baha'i Writings, Baha'u'llah, Gleanings From the Writings of Baha'u'llah, pg. 285

–Lisa

List five events in your life and how you benefited from the hardship.

1.
2.
3.
4.
5.

List five events when you were of service to someone and how that felt.

1.
2.
3.
4.
5.

WEEK 47

Strength. We all fight so hard to be seen as strong. To have the appearance of being "put together"

We all wish we were better moms, wives, daughters, sisters, friends and children of God. We second guess and wring our hands. We compare ourselves to others constantly. What if I told you, woman to woman, it's ok to not be perfect?

It is okay to be weak and struggle sometimes. Actually, it is more than okay, especially when Christ's power is made perfect within you. In 2 Corinthians, Paul talks about struggling with a thorn in his flesh. He begged God for help, and God responded.

2 Corinthians 12: 8-10(ESV) "Three times I pleaded with the Lord about this, that it should leave me. But he said to me, 'My grace is sufficient for you, for my power is made perfect in weakness.' Therefore, I will boast all the more gladly of my weaknesses, so that the power of Christ may rest upon me. For the sake of Christ, then, I am content with weaknesses, insults, hardships, persecutions, and calamities. For when I am weak, then I am strong."

I hope this Scripture calms your heart, as it does mine. To know I can trust in God's strength and that his grace is sufficient gives me permission to rest. It's permission to not be perfect. When we are weak, we are strong. That sounds strange, but it is true. Don't worry about being strong or perfect. Rest. Rest in the grace and power of Christ upon you. Peace be with you today.

–Kristie Romano

Name 5 weaknesses that you beat yourself up over. How does that make you feel?

1.
2.
3.
4.
5.

How do you feel when you learn to accept your faults and love all parts of yourself?

Week 48

"God loves us too much to answer our prayer at any other time than the right time and in any other way than the right way."

–Terkeurst, Lysa. "LysaTerkeurst.com". 2018 www.lysaterkeurst.com/2018/10/why-isnt-god-answering-my-prayer-2/

I was overwhelmed. I had little sleep and little patience left. I love my students, but they were driving me absolutely crazy! I had retaught the expectations of the classroom almost every day and answered the same math question about five times that hour, and then I lost it. I don't remember what I said, but I do remember what I heard.

"Britnie, am I this impatient with you?"

I had never heard His voice so clearly before that moment. I know I am not the most patient person, but wow did I need that wakeup call. The answer is no, He is never that impatient with me. I get frustrated when I feel like I am trying so hard and my plans do not work. I'm not where I think I should be; this is not what I pictured. Then, I get angry with God.

Unlike me in that moment, He doesn't lash out at me when I ask the same questions over and over again. He doesn't get angry when I question Him or forget that He is always right next to me. He listens, He guides and He loves me through my impatience.

He leads me to His word or a song and reminds me of His promises of all good things that come in time and through lessons.

When I feel impatient or overwhelmed or disappointed, I remember that God has the plan. He teaches me like I teach my students. It is not about the grade I receive for what I do right or wrong, but the lessons I learn along the way. The biggest lesson being to trust and listen to Him. When I learn to trust Him, I remember that He has the best timing and only the best waiting for me. Like Lysa Terkeurst says, He loves me too much to give me anything at any other time than His perfect timing.

–Britnie

Name 5 events in your life that you wanted immediate answers about from God. When you did not get them, how did that make you feel?

1.
2.
3.
4.
5.

How did the event turn out when you waited on God's timing?

Week 49

The Courage of Waiting

There are many types of heroes. They are amazing individuals and animals who have shown great courage in the face of danger or sudden peril, like the brave and skilled first responders we see in the news. Sometimes, heroes have spoken up for others' rights or defended the innocent. We greatly admire those willingly putting themselves on the line to help others. How courageous they are! But I have discovered that there is another type of great courage. It's found in Psalms 27:13-14(KJV). The courage of... waiting.

"I had fainted, unless I had believed to see the goodness of the LORD in the land of the living. Wait on the LORD: be of good courage, and he shall strengthen thine heart: wait, I say, on the LORD."

This type of courage is built on inactivity, and it sounds like a contradiction! Aren't the brave always those who "do" something!

I realized I HAVE seen this type of courage before. In my mother who waited patiently for my military father to come home from overseas. In people's faces waiting in hospital rooms, supporting those they care about. In friends who shared strength when my father passed away. These unsung heroes are also the first to shout for joy when a degree is earned, or a child is born.

We are called by the Lord to "be of good courage" and to "wait on him." We are directed to patiently trust rather than do in times of unsolvable adversity. We are to keep believing not only that God's unfailing love will be there with us, but also that he will strengthen our hearts through our circumstances. This type of courage makes BIG headlines in heaven.

What good things or outcomes from God are you waiting for today? You're my hero!

–Ann Kincaid

Name 5 situations when you were forced to wait on something and could not take control.

1.
2.
3.
4.
5.

Name the outcome when you waited and didn't jump in and try to take control.

Week 50

Amazing Grace

By the age of thirty, I had everything I could ever want. In no particular order, I had earned my doctoral degree in psychology and I had a great job, a wonderful family, a marriage that looked perfect, two precious kids, a home, a church I was involved with, and good friends. I made friends easily, and my job as a professional—as well as my family's influence, generosity, and hospitality in our local town—afforded me a position of respect and honor in my community. I recall saying when I was around the age of twenty-seven, that if I died tomorrow, I would have everything that I ever wanted. I was happy. Content. Grateful. I loved life, and life loved me. Life had always come pretty easily for me. From the outside, I had everything a woman could want.

Life changed for me when I began having an affair with a mutual family friend after nine years of marriage. You should know I had never so much looked at another man in my entire life. I had two long-term boyfriends before I met my husband and considered myself a loyal person. I was hardly the type who had a wandering eye. The affair started innocently enough as two friends working out together, but it quickly turned into an emotional affair and then eventually physical. Within twelve months of the start of this relationship, I lost everything. My boys were two and three when my husband and I divorced. I went from being a hands-on mom to seeing my toddlers half of the week. I moved out of my lovely house in the sweet cul-de-sac where we lived, and moved into a house that had been abandoned for more than a year. To call it a fixer upper would be a compliment. My family was so angry and hurt with me that they stopped talking to me. Literally. For months. I brought shame on my family, who had always prided themselves on their good name, our good family and our reputation. My church family turned away. I found out years later the pastor of the church I had been attending used my name in a board meeting as an example of what not to be. My friends took my husband's side and turned away from me. My reputation very quickly became "Homewrecker." "Cheater." "Slut." Because of my guilt, I did not want to ask for child support. I made very little money at the time, so I went from being relatively comfortable, to being broke. To say I was broken and alone is an understatement.

But God.

After realizing very quickly that my church home did not afford me the safety and hospitality I so desperately needed, I began attending a large church in a large city where nobody knew me, nobody knew my story, and I could cry or worship in peace. Without judgment. It was the only place I felt safe, because I thought I could hide. Despite my sin and the hurtful ways that people responded to me, I knew God still was there. He showed up in very real and tangible ways over the next few years. He pursued me.

This devotional is not long enough to share with you all of the ways He showed me His amazing grace. How He provided me with a $30,000 grant to fix up my house, along with other blessings.

Shortly after I started attending this new church, the pastor started a series called "Family Mess." The series after Family Mess was one highlighting the major sinners of the Bible and how the Lord uses them: stories of David, Rahab, Moses, and Paul. Flawed people who shared the Lord's heart. I began to see myself in a different way. In a very personal way, the Lord was telling me my brokenness and sin was no match for His Grace. Over time, he restored and transformed my family. My brother, who is now a pastor, said, "Your divorce was the worst thing and the best thing that ever could have happened to our family." He has restored my faith in marriage. Healthy marriage. I married the person I had the affair with, and between the two of us, we have five children ranging in age from five to twenty-five. By God's grace, they have relationships with us, with each other and with the Lord. It has been remarkable to sit back and watch how He has even moved in their lives despite the dumb choices their parents made. My private practice as a psychologist has grown exponentially, and a big part of my job is being able to walk alongside other people who are broken or who are walking through broken relationships. Shame has been transformed to testimony. God was bigger than my shame. He was bigger than my aloneness. He is bigger than my brokenness. He showed me that He loved me when I was unlovable. He was there when everyone else had abandoned me. He blessed me when I deserved punishment. He exalted me when I was lowly. Sitting there in that pew, in that big church, I sang the words to "Amazing Grace" as tears rolled down my cheeks. I have sung that song one thousand times over the course of my life, but that day it was as if I was hearing it for the first time.

> *Amazing Grace, How Sweet the Sound*
> *That Saved a wretch like me.*
> *I once was lost but now I am found.*
> *'Twas blind but now I see.*
>
> –Newton, John. "Amazing Grace". Olney Hymns. England, 1779.

–Amynda Rhodes

Name events or choices in your life you were not proud of, and the consequences you faced as a result.

How did you learn to forgive yourself and move on from these experiences?

Week 51

"It is when I struggle, I strengthen. It is when challenged to my core, I learn the depth of who I am."

–Maraboli, Steve. "Unapologetically You: Reflections on Life and the Human Experience". New York: Better Today Publishing, 2013

As women, we struggle through more than most ever know. We put on a brave face for all who depend on us. We put one foot in front of the other and do what we need done. We get up early and go to bed late. Sometimes our office chairs and seats in the car are the only places for us to sit during a day. We think we are in it alone sometimes and that we have to internalize and deal with our problems alone. We feel that we have to live up to the expectations of others and that letting people see us struggle makes us weak. I am so thankful I learned that isn't true. My own life had its struggles that likely mirror many others.

Getting teased on a bus for developing young, growing up in a broken home, dealing with heartbreak, losing friends too young, getting divorced, losing "friends" again, unwanted career changes, muddling through single motherhood, dating after eighteen years... Then rising above, smiling in the face of a bully, helping my family through the tough times, leaning on a friend's shoulder, having a soul-cleansing cry, becoming an even better mother, learning who my true friends are, and learning and loving who I am. Struggle and strengthen. That's what we do. We are women, we are mothers, we are daughters, we are friends. We struggle, we learn and we improve. If not for adversity, would we be who we are now? Would we be the strong, amazing, independent, loving women we are?

I say thanks for the struggles that strengthened me.

–Andrea

Name 5 challenges that have tested you to the core.

1.
2.
3.
4.
5.

Name how those challenges have strengthened you.

Week 52

Continue

I believe the universe puts people in our lives to teach us, to guide us, to love us and to sometimes leave us. These relationships must manifest organically so that both souls can become who they are supposed to become, because they were authentically loved by the other soul. A random encounter turned into a life-changing friendship because he helped me find the courage to continue. The quote below is a text message from my friend Brian during one of my darkest moments. I read this text every day and allowed the words to transform me. I survived human trafficking, domestic violence, suicide, and homelessness because he believed in me when I couldn't believe in myself.

"When your clouds feel negative and unbalanced, give time to step outside your light to take a look at what it is doing to you. Let it speak to you, but size it up and flatten it out with knowledge. You have the answer Jessica, you have the right energy and you have the charm to beat it with a smile. Let your forces shine love; nothing, or no one person or persons, has the power to make you unbalanced or bring you into a negative light. Continue, Jessica, tell yourself this word when you feel this way. Just say it out loud love, continue. I believe in my friend. I know my friend has clarity. I know she can do whatever she desires. Love what is right in your light Jessica. It won't be easy when you are on a natural path of change because those negative forces want to pull you down with them. I love what I see in you. I love what I feel from you, Jessica, and I know what you want for yourself. Continue Jessica, continue."

Continue has become my mantra. It is tattooed on my wrist as a reminder that no matter how hard life gets, continue. We all have that courage to continue, but sometimes we need people to believe in us until we can believe in ourselves again.

–Jessica Kay Halling

Name 5 people who came into your life and the lessons they taught you.

1.
2.
3.
4.
5.

Name 5 people whom you could reach out to with an inspiring message.

1.
2.
3.
4.
5.

Bonus Devotionals

Bonus Week 1

What if Jesus wrote a devotional?

I wondered, if Jesus wrote a devotional for this book, what would it say? As I pondered my question, I could hear Jesus saying this:

"I spent my whole life preparing for Easter Sunday, along the way, I had ups and downs, but what got me through was trust in my father, that he would bring me back to heaven. I was a baby born in a manger, growing up in a family who was made fun of, and I got in trouble with my mom and dad when I decided to stay in the city while they looked for me. It took them a few days to find me, not knowing if I was kidnapped or lost.

But at that time, being a teenager, I thought I knew everything. See, my life is not so different from all of you, but I chose good, not bad. I did not have a Starbucks every morning to get me through the day, but I had the "silence" to find my faith. I did belong to a gang, formed by the twelve apostles, but we did not terrorize; we offered kindness and food to people, although we might have thought we were hot stuff, traveling all around talking to crowds. So, my advice to you is to tell yourself you are so precious because you are, and do some good because it will make me look good to my Father."

Thanks, Jesus

–V

Name 5 events in your life when you thought you knew everything and handled them your way.

1.
2.
3.
4.
5.

How could you have followed Jesus's footsteps and handled those situations differently?

____

____

____

____

____

____

____

____

____

____

Bonus Week 2

Grow, share your gifts, and give the rest to God.

Like many of you, I could be called a victim. A victim of abuse, an unstable home environment, no father, broken relationships, money issues, bad decisions, bad luck, bad people, and on and on. Today, forty-some years later, you may be surprised by my back story. Today, I am blessed with a great husband, a healthy marriage, two amazing children, stability, a successful career and great friends and family. It has been a journey, with so many failures and life lessons learned. It all started with an honest look in the mirror and a challenge to myself to be better, and to seek the best for my family, friends and community.

Don't let your issues define you. We all have friends who haven't gotten past a defining negative moment in their life—a past insult, trauma, or tragedy. They obsess about the wrong things, talk about their acquaintances, make snarky comments and envy the lives of others. Don't be that person! Make peace with whatever person or issue may be troubling you, and let go of stale dreams and bitter emotions. Making peace with those issues will set you free! I learned a long time ago that the only person I was hurting by holding on to the past was myself. Give yourself and others a little grace. We all have baggage in life; it's all about how we decide to transport it.

"There is no future, there is no past. I live this moment as my last."

–Larson, Jonathan. "Another Day." Rent, Warner Records, 2005, track 10

Share your gifts. God gave everyone a gift, and it is our responsibility to share it with others. Make time to discover what your gift is, seek input from friends and pray. Whether your gift is creativity, time, love for animals, work ethic or even the gift of gab, find an outlet to share your talents with others. By giving your time and treasures to others who are in need, you will receive more than you ever imagined. I started volunteering during my paper route in fourth grade, when I met the residents of a nursing home who received the daily paper. While spending time with the residents, I tried my best to absorb their wisdom like a sponge, and I am a different person today because of the experience. We share the gift of volunteerism with our children by helping people at a homeless shelter, delivering Meals on Wheels and encouraging the boys to use their birthday parties to raise money for the wish fulfillment of a sick child. Imagine a world in which we all donate an hour a week to helping others—the world would be a brighter and kinder place.

> *"Life's most persistent and urgent question is, 'What are you doing for others?'" –Dr. Marin Luther King Jr.*
>
> –King Jr., Dr. Martin Luther."Martin Luther King, Jr. Quotes." BrainyQuote.com BrainyMedia Inc, 2020. www.brainyquote.com/quotes/martin luther king jr 137105

Be your own cheerleader. I have had many failures, disappointments and tragedy in my life. I could easily wallow in those moments, feel sorry for myself or seek revenge. Instead, I choose joy. In order to be happy and fulfilled in life, we need to come to terms with our issues and be our biggest cheerleader. Don't allow your inner critic to take control and drive; drown it out with positive and kind messages to yourself. Find peace with those who have wronged you, and find self-forgiveness for your past mistakes, and your energy will attract happiness and success. Don't be surprised if this takes a lot of work! Try tangible but achievable activities you can develop into habits: speak or write daily gratitude's, pray or meditate for fifteen minutes, find an exercise you like and spend time with positive people.

> *"Watch your thoughts, they become your words; watch your words, they become your actions; watch your actions, they become your habits; watch your habits, they become your character; watch your character, it becomes your destiny."*
>
> –Commonly attributed to Lao Tzu in the third century. www.medium.com/mindset-matters/who-said-watch-your-thoughts-they-become-your-words-d645dff454b8

Give our worries and the glory to God. As a "type A" person, I have lived my life by trying to control my environment and outcomes. When facing one of my life's greatest challenges, I realized it was a situation over which I had no control. It was affecting me and everyone around me. In this situation, I felt betrayed and wronged, and the issue began to consume me. I had always heard people say, "Give it to God and let it go," and I really never knew how to embrace that concept. "Letting go" didn't seem possible, nor was that in my nature. When the pressures became overwhelming and I had nowhere else to turn, I thought I would give it a try, as I didn't have much to lose. I told myself that any time I thought about the issue, I would pray and think about something else. After just a few short days (and a LOT of prayer), I was shocked by how quickly the burden was lessened, and I experienced this overwhelming sense of love and calm. While I have to remind myself often to give it to God (often multiple times a day), doing so has helped me realize He is in the driver's seat, and I don't need to sweat the small stuff. It has helped in my relationships, work and overall life.

During this low point, I contemplated hate and anger and wanted to expose the offending party. I knew the high road was the only way to go. With prayer and clinging to promises in Scriptures like the one below, amazing things started to take off in my life. I knew this was all God! Nothing changed in my abilities or contributions, but the simple flip in my focus and release to God as my defender and vindicator resulted in the best outcome, which I could have never anticipated. A dear friend asked how I was doing so well, as she knew the situation, and I simply replied, "All the glory goes to God."

"Do not fret because of those who are evil or be envious of those who do wrong; for like the grass they will soon wither, like green plants they will soon die away. Trust in the Lord and do good; dwell in the land and enjoy safe pasture. Take delight in the Lord, and he will give you the desires of your heart.

Commit your way to the Lord; trust in him and he will do this: He will make your righteous reward shine like the dawn, your vindication like the noonday sun. Be still before the Lord and wait patiently for him; do not fret when people succeed in their ways, when they carry out their wicked schemes. Refrain from anger and turn from wrath; do not fret—it leads only to evil. For those who are evil will be destroyed, but those who hope in the Lord will inherit the land." Psalms 37: 1-9(NIV)

–Laura

Name past or current issues you are letting define you, as a person. How does it make you feel?

____

____

____

____

____

____

____

____

Name ways you can make peace with these issues by believing in yourself and giving your worries to your higher power.

Bonus Week 3

The Battle is Not Yours

No doubt, as women, we find ourselves every day on the frontline. Right there, we face life's challenging situations with our backs up against insurmountable odds.

How often do we examine our lives and find our relationships in disarray, finances on life support, questioning our purpose and wrestling nonstop with our next move in life?

As an ordained pastor alongside my husband, a mom of two adult children, a business owner, an international author and a speaker, I have had to deal with many challenges and the silence of God.

Admit, there is something wrong.

I will never forget during a cruise vacation, I sat on the balcony with a mimosa, starting to question God after not hearing from Him for a long time. A funny thing during this time of silence is that I was able to pray for others, and their requests were answered, but the moment I prayed for myself, I heard absolutely nothing. I remember saying to my husband, "Babe, I am struggling right now. I am starting to question my Christianity. I am a little scared being that I am someone who is upfront speaking to people about the Lord and inviting them into the family of God, yet I have questions forming after months of silence from Jesus." My husband replied, "You're in a good place." What? I'm sure I looked at him with frustration, but he was right.

You see, I was in a battle. I had remained silent, keeping the way I was feeling inside, trying my best not to say anything negative about God or the way I was feeling. However, after tapping into my boldness and saying those words out loud, it was as though the mask came off, and I was able to hear God through His silence.

We are faced with internal battles. In my case, it was God's silence. We read in II Chronicles 20:17 (NIV) that "You will not have to fight this battle. Take up your positions; stand firm and see the deliverance the Lord will give you..."

It may appear that God is missing in action, but if you stay the course, you can look back to see where God came along and swooped you up and carried you to safety. Even in the silence, know that God is near and waiting for you to admit there is something wrong. That battle is not yours; it's the Lord's.

–Gail Dudley

Name times in your life when you felt like your prayers weren't being answered and how you felt.

____

____

____

____

____

Now that time has passed, can you look back and see that God never left you, and how he may have carried you during those rough times?

____

____

____

____

____

Bonus Week 4

Do what you gotta do to get through

To me, doing what you gotta do is about knowing who you are, working hard, loving harder and living your best life—the best way you know how.

Growing up, my family and home life was less than desirable. We were crammed into a cluttered, little house with no privacy or personal space. Day in and day out, I was "boxed in" by negative energy, constant arguing and perpetual uncertainty about whether we had enough money for basic needs, let alone wants. I was forced to formulate happiness and stay hopeful that when I got out of that house, I would create life the way I wanted it to be.

Throughout my journey, I have been fortunate to have had, and still have, incredibly strong, genuine, solid relationships with some amazing people. These relationships are paramount! It would have been impossible to get to where I am today without the love and support from my circle of friends and relationships. I will be forever indebted to the special peeps in my life, and I owe thousands of dollars in Girlfriend Therapy!

And let's just say I am a bit of a spirited gal. A little fiery, a lot goofy and very energetic (ok and a big splash of ADHD!). Humor has been my "go-to" in getting me through. And nothing beats a good, deep belly laugh, which I try to sprinkle a little bit of wherever I go.

So, the moral to my story is that I tap in to what I have: relationships, humor and wine—ha!, and do what I need to do to shape what I want out of life.

Some coping skills that have helped me get through life are: blasting tunes, texting my girlfriends, walking, and driving in my car with my butt warmer on and my sunroof open in any weather! These might sound silly, but those little acts really help clear my brain.

I have come to realize no one can really "make you" happy, think, be or do anything. You are the only one who creates your own destiny. You are the only one who knows how to adapt and recalibrate in order to get through to where you need to be.

So, the operative word to my little mantra is: you!

–Anonymous

Name 5 coping skills you have developed that help you make it through your tough times.

1.
2.
3.
4.
5.

Name new skills you can develop to help you adjust to new challenges in your life.

Conclusion

I hope these inspiring stories have touched your heart and let you know that you're not alone. We all have our stories, walk through hardships, and in the end come out stronger than before!

Many thanks again to all of you for purchasing this book! Your purchase has helped in the fight against sex trafficking.

To be a part of the next book, "Fierce Woman from Around the World", please send your stories to fiercewomentoday@gmail.com. You will find details on how to submit your stories at
www.fiercewomentoday.com

Now go Be the Fierce Woman you were meant to Be!

Why I Wrote Fierce Woman Inspirational

I feel like I have been guided on this lifelong path to write this book for some time now. I see how the Lord has led me from the health care field helping cancer patients as a radiation therapist to owning my own day spa and helping women feel more beautiful. I have always connected with women on a deep spiritual level and could feel their happiness as well as their hurts.

Most recently I have been involved with women's charities who work to combat sex trafficking. After hearing the horrific stories my heart was deeply touched and I knew I had to do something to help make a difference in this world. Human trafficking is a multi-billion-dollar criminal industry that steals the victim's freedom and, in some cases, physically forces victims to sell sex and work under inhumane and unacceptable conditions.

We as woman must stand up for those who cannot help themselves and give them hope and love.

So, with the sale of this book I will be donating a portion of the proceeds to charities that help fight against sex trafficking. My hope is to bring more awareness to this modern-day sex slavery.

Natalie

Fierce Woman Poem

"The Fierce Woman"

She is bold and strong with a smile that keeps going on and on

She laughs as though her soul is being expressed and she tends
to draw out people's best

When she encounters troubles and sorrows in her life she
bends and winds like a river around the strife

Her aura and infectious smile draw you in and you feel at
home once again!

If you are fortunate enough to be loved by this woman my
friend, then She will be your confidant until the end

When your heart aches, her heart cries as you connect on a
spiritual level through her eyes.

So, all you beautiful women dig deep down inside and find
the fierceness that resides and let the light of you shine free

Bring it for the world to see and "be the first woman you were
meant to be!"

–Natalie Blake

Reflections

About the Author

I am a fierce woman!
I can roar like a lion but also have a powerfully, sappy side to me as well.
I feel the hurts of other women, and I am eager to come alongside to empower and inspire.
I am a part of a sisterhood of fierceness that connects one to another and grows leaps and bounds.

I believe nothing makes a woman more beautiful than a big, bright smile and a bold infectious laugh!

My name? I am Natalie.

Natalie Blake.

An Ohioan.

Day Spa owner.

Vacation rental property owner.

Natty Girl Handbag Company founder.

I am that author whose mission is to uplift others. My first book, "The Fierce Woman Inspirational," will showcase everyday women with inspiring life stories.

I am a proud wife, mother, and even grandmother to a beautiful, sassy little granddaughter who keeps her Gigi hopping!

That's me!

Natalie

Now for the Traditional Bio:

Natalie Blake is a serial entrepreneur, owner/esthetician of Willow Tree Day Spa, co-founder of the Natty Girl Company specializing an Italian leather handbags, and vacation rental property owner.

Through my 20 years of owning my day spa, I have connected with numerous inspirational women where they have shared their life stories. These amazing stories have motivated me to write a 52-week inspirational featuring inspiring women. This book is designed to inspire, uplift and encourage other women.

To connect with Natalie and learn how you can contribute with your own fierce story, please visit her website at www.fiercewomentoday.com

CPSIA information can be obtained
at www.ICGtesting.com
Printed in the USA
FSHW020633260321

9 781735 807317